MOONSHINERS
& REVENUERS

To Robert & Brenda,

Hope you enjoy the
READ !.

Merry Christmas !

Johny Berkley

12/2020

It's been so long now
But it seems now, that it was only yesterday
Gee, ain't it funny, how time slips away

–Willie Nelson, 1961

CONTENTS

INTRODUCTION

"Find a job you enjoy doing, and you will never have to work a day in your life" is a quote attributed to Mark Twain.

I was fortunate to find such a job as a Special Agent with the Bureau of Alcohol, Tobacco and Firearms (ATF), U.S. Treasury Department. Throughout most of my 25-year career with ATF (1969–1994), I looked forward to and enjoyed going to work most every day. Each day seemed to bring something new, interesting, exciting and challenging.

In 1969 when I started in Raleigh, North Carolina, ATF's mission was the enforcement of federal liquor laws and regulations— catching moonshiners and seizing and destroying their liquor distilleries and moonshine whiskey. Although moonshining was declining, there were still hotbeds of activity and many moonshine stills operating in the counties worked by the Raleigh ATF office. As the years passed, however, moonshining and the illegal liquor business continued to decline to the point that in the late 1970s the federal government no longer considered it a significant problem requiring federal attention. As a result, ATF refocused its priorities placing liquor enforcement at the very bottom of its priority list. It was during this period that ATF went from a division of the Internal Revenue Service to an independent Bureau within the U.S. Treasury Department.

With the birth of the new Bureau in 1972, major changes began to take place both in terms of personnel as well as organizational and enforcement priorities. The most drastic change was the aforementioned retreat from liquor enforcement and the personnel changes made as a result. Small "liquor offices" throughout the Southeast, including those in North Carolina, were closed and the personnel moved to larger offices, primarily to Chicago, Washington, and Boston. Not only did the priorities change, the entire organizational structure and the very culture of ATF changed.

The regional structure under the IRS was eliminated, and ATF became a re-purposed organization with Washington at the top and "in charge". Emphasis was placed on the enforcement of federal firearms and explosives laws, and for brief periods the federal laws on wagering and cigarette smuggling. Under the explosive's statutes, arson—and particularly arson-for-profit—became a major priority. The National Response Team (NRT) concept was developed to address major fires and explosives incidences and was successful to the point that ATF became recognized as the premier agency in investigating large scale fires and explosives incidents.

Although the changing landscape of the agency was necessary for its survival and was successful in the long run, there was much agony and pain along the way. The upheaval associated with the 1976 closing of the "liquor offices" and re-deployment of personnel was very painful and traumatic to the affected agents and their families who were "forced" to leave their homes and move to unfamiliar—and for some—a seemingly foreign culture and way of life. The legitimacy and very existence of the agency was challenged a number of times resulting in efforts to abolish ATF. The most serious and real "abolish ATF" threat occurred in 1982 after the election of conservative President Ronald Reagan.

The National Rifle Association (NRA), which had long been at odds with ATF over the enforcement of the federal firearms laws, saw with the new President an opportunity to abolish ATF and greatly reduce or even eliminate the enforcement of the hated Gun Control Act of 1968. With its allies in Congress and elsewhere, plans were formulated to abolish ATF and transfer its personnel and laws to other agencies, primarily to the Secret Service. Unlike on other occasions, this effort was more than just a rumor—it was real, and it was going to happen. The Charlotte Assistant Special Agent in Charge announced at a district-wide meeting, "it is a done deal". We actually received written notice of Reduction in Force (your job is being eliminated). The information was not just coming from within ATF, the local Secret Service office also requested information as to personnel and equipment at the Raleigh ATF office. It did not happen, but there would be other attempts to disband ATF. But the agency survived the changes, missteps, problems and challenges of its infant years and today is a much larger organization within the Department of Justice.

From my vantage point, primarily in North Carolina, I was both a participant in and witness to the evolution of ATF from its moonshine days to the multi-jurisdictional federal law enforcement agency it has become. Admittedly, those first seven or eight years working the moonshiners were the most enjoyable and satisfying. I have so many fond memories of that time, and as I reflect back, I am so thankful to have been a part of "the days of moonshiners and revenuers."

One might ask how being out in the woods, sometimes for days, dealing with the heat, cold, snow, rain, mosquitoes, red bugs, Vienna sausages, Nabs crackers, and beanie-weenies, could in anyway be enjoyable. I suppose it is like a lot of things, if you haven't been there or done it, you really can't understand it.

Over the course of my career, I participated in numerous narcotics, firearms, and explosives raids and arrests, but none compare with the excitement and exhilaration of a moonshine still raid. You've lain out in the woods two or three days, and then early in the morning you hear the sound of an old truck slowly approaching up the still road. It stops in the still yard, and you soon hear sounds and see movements in and about the still. As you give the still hands a few minutes to get settled in and go about their work, the excitement and anticipation build, and the adrenalin starts pumping as you slowly inch up closer to the still. Then you hear "Federal agent—you are under arrest!" and all hell breaks loose and the chase is on. Most of the time we were able to run down and arrest the fleeing moonshiners, but some times they got away. It has been said that all good things must come to an end, and it did. The era of the moonshiners and revenuers, which had lasted many decades in the Southeastern U.S., was for the most part over. It was time to move on.

Most of us were able to, and did, move on and adjust to the changing ATF as it struggled to transition from moonshine to guns and explosives, but there were still a few of the "old revenuers" who could not, and did not. Fortunately, most were near retirement age and they were allowed to just mark time until they reached retirement. Some of the younger agents, however, just quit rather than make the move to Chicago and the other large urban cities. They were replaced in large numbers by younger agents who, unfortunately, never experienced the moonshine days, and their only knowledge was from what they read or the stories from "the old timers". No more chasing moonshiners, it was now chasing gun runners, felons with guns, drug dealers with guns, bombers, arsonists, and cigarette smugglers. The Bloods, Crips, Hells Angels, Jamaican drug gangs, and other organized and often unorganized gangs and violent criminals became the focus of ATF's attention. And that is what I did for the remainder of my career with the exception of a couple forays into management.

This book is the story of my 25-year career with ATF from 1969 until 1994, the period wherein ATF transitioned from being "the redheaded stepchild of the IRS" working moonshine whiskey, to the multi-jurisdictional independent bureau it has become. More than just a history with facts and dates, it is about the people (good guys and bad guys), events, situations, and places I encountered along the way, as well as my observations and thoughts.

I wrote this book because I think it is an important story that should be told and told from the point of view of one with some firsthand knowledge. The era of the moonshiners, a way of life and culture of a people that had existed for decades, was over.

This book is based on a few documents and papers I have held onto over the years (through many moves and a major fire), some research, conversations with former agents, and to a great extent on my memory of people and events. As I get older, I sometimes can't remember things that happened last week or even yesterday, but I can remember most every still we seized including its location, size, and who we caught.

I realize in the current cultural climate that mandates we strive for diversity and inclusiveness, where the phobia of offending someone or some group—and political correctness in general—is ever present, some readers may consider parts or all of this book to be offensive, insensitive, biased, crude, racist, sexist, and all the other "ists" in today's culture. But I ask that it be viewed, to the extent possible, through the lens of that time, place, and people. It was a time when there were no computers, Internet, smart phones, tablets, iPads, GPS devices, or Google. It was a much simpler day and, for better or worse, a very different time and way of seeing and doing things.

MOONSHINERS & REVENUERS

From Bootleggers to Arsonists — ATF's Battle Against Criminals in North Carolina

Part One

MOONSHINERS & REVENUERS
(1969 - 1978)

PREFACE

With the passage of the 21st Amendment in 1933, Prohibition ended in the United States. It was once again legal to manufacture, distribute and sell liquor. However, in most southern states the Amendment was not immediately ratified and the prohibition remained in effect.

In North Carolina the amendment was ratified in 1937, at which time the Alcohol Beverage Control (ABC) system was set up to regulate the distribution and sale of alcohol. It wasn't until 1979 that legal liquor distilleries were allowed in North Carolina. Under the ABC system, municipalities and counties were allowed to vote on whether or not they wanted ABC liquor stores within their boundaries. Some of the more-populated urban towns and counties approved the establishment of ABC liquor stores, but most of the more-rural counties did not. Thusly, most of North Carolina counties remained dry—that is the legal sale of liquor was prohibited. In North Carolina it was said that the Baptist and the bootlegger vote kept legal alcohol outlets out of most counties.

While the sale of alcohol was still prohibited and suppressed in North Carolina and most southern states, the appetite and demand for it was not. And as with most commodities, when there is a demand there will be a supply. For more than four decades the moonshiners in North Carolina and throughout the Southeastern states provided that commodity in abundance. There were still small-time moonshiners who continued to make a little for family and friends, but the vast majority of moonshine liquor was made "to sell" and a lot of it was made, sold and consumed.

Chapter One

THE BEGINNING

M y story begins in the spring of 1969, while in my senior year at Pembroke State University. With the expectation to graduate at the end of summer school (contingent on my passing the required twelve hours of foreign language), I had started to think about a job after graduation. Majoring in political science and history, my initial thoughts were going into teaching at the high school level or perhaps law enforcement. Professor Adolph Dial, my academic advisor, suggested that I apply to the North Carolina State Bureau of Investigation (SBI), which at that time was a relatively small agency but was about to expand and hire a significant number of new agents.

Professor Dial was into Democratic politics, and since the Democrats controlled everything in N.C., he felt that he could put a good word in for me. At about the same time, an army CID investigator friend told me that he had a friend with the Secret Service and could get me an interview. I was interviewed by the Secret Service Supervisor in Charlotte, who said they had no openings at the time but suggested I go ahead and take the entry test. While he seemed pleased with the interview, he did mention that the Secret Service had a weight/height requirement and the fact that I was vertically challenged (short) might be an issue. But I took, and passed, the Treasury Enforcement Agent exam.

A few weeks later, I received a letter from the Alcohol, Tobacco and Firearms Division of the Internal Revenue Service (ATFD) informing me they were hiring new investigators and asking me to come to Raleigh for an interview. I really didn't know much about the ATFD, but I must admit growing up in Chatham County in the '50s and '60s, I had heard the term "Federal ATU Man". *Could they be the one and the same?*

As I recall, there were three or four interviewers including Marvin Shaw and M.L. Goodwin from the Regional Office. The interview went well, apparently, as I was "unofficially" offered a job pending my graduating in August. Asked to list my top three duty station preferences, I listed in order 1) Fayetteville (I was living there), 2) Raleigh and 3) Charlotte. I was told that chances were not good to get any of the three, as it was policy to assign new investigators outside their home state. After graduating in August, I received written notification that I was hired, and my duty station would be Raleigh. I was told to report to the Charlotte District office on September 8th.

On Monday morning, September 8, 1969, at 7:45 am, I reported to the ATFD District Office in Charlotte, NC, to be sworn in as a Special Investigator. Special Investigator in Charge Jarvis Brewer administered the oath and the balance of that day and half the next was spent going through orientation, signing forms, and qualifying with the revolver issued to me. Agnes Hunter, Secretary to the SIC, handled most of the paperwork and Assistant Special Investigator in Charge John Wurtele and Raleigh Area Supervisor D.C. Lawson handled most of the non-paper orientation.

Special Investigator Stan Noel issued me a revolver and set of handcuffs, and drove me to the range in the basement of the Federal Reserve building to train and qualify me with the revolver. I recall being told how to load, aim and shoot the gun, and firing either six or twelve rounds. Whichever, I qualified and was duly authorized to carry and use the weapon. The orientation was completed shortly after lunch on Tuesday, at which time I drove to Raleigh, my assigned post of duty (POD). The following morning at 7:30 am, I reported to the Raleigh office to begin my twenty-five-year ATF career.

The Raleigh office was located in the IRS building on North Street, a few blocks north of the Governor's mansion and a couple blocks south of the Krispy Cream Doughnut store. Area Supervisor D.C. Lawson showed me around and introduced me to the other investigators in the office: Bobby Sherrill, Don Devaney, Bill Walden, Tommy Stokes and Bill Brawley. I learned that Sherrill had been there for some time, but the others were relatively new arrivals like myself. Devaney had transferred in from the Border Patrol, Walden and Stokes had just transferred in from Alabama and Georgia respectively, and Brawley was a new hire. I also met

Joe Carter and Ed Gray, Atlanta Regional Special Investigators working out of the Raleigh POD. Betty Haley was the new office secretary and it was her first day on the job, too. Michael Zetts, the Investigator in Charge, was away on a fishing trip and not scheduled to return until the next week.

Shortly after getting to the office, Special Investigator Walden informed me that he and I, as well as Special Investigator Stokes and Brawley, were going to Wilkesboro. I had heard of Wilkesboro and Wilkes County as being the "moonshine capital", so I was pretty excited about working in Wilkesboro my first day. But, my excitement was dampened a bit when I was told we were going there to pick up some desks for the office. The Wilkesboro POD, located in the basement of the federal building, like Raleigh, was preparing for a wave of newly hired investigators. They were getting new desks and office equipment and giving us some of their old ones. I couldn't figure why they were getting the new stuff and giving us the old stuff. After all, Raleigh was the capital city and described by some as "the garden spot of ATF". It was the first of many "I wonder why" mysteries that I would experience during my career. So, my first day as a Special Investigator, I moved desk and office equipment (and would do so several more times in my career).

Mr. Zetts returned from his fishing trip the following Monday and told me to come into his office. Mike was a large man, originally from Pennsylvania I believe. He played football at the University of Maryland under Bear Bryant, I was told. Mike was very direct—often blunt—and characterized as "a bull in a China shop". I remember vividly that shortly after I walked into his office the first time, he looked me over (I was 5'7" and weighed maybe 140 lbs.) and said, "Boy do you know karate or something? Because if you don't, some damn big bootlegger is going to beat the hell out of you".

I told him I didn't and he just shook his head. Unlike Mike, D.C. appeared to be very smooth and a bit more tactful. I was told that D.C. was a decorated Marine in WWII and still carried shrapnel from wounds received during battle of Okinawa.

Although I was eager to get to work in the field, it was Mike's policy that new investigators with no prior law enforcement experience really didn't do much until they had completed training. So, my first few days were pretty much limited to riding with various investigators, learning the territory and meeting state and local officers.

Off to School

In September 1969, I reported to Washington, DC to begin my initial training in Treasury Law Enforcement Officers Training School (TELOTS). There was no federal law enforcement training center as is the case now in Glynco, Georgia. My class consisted of approximately sixty new agents from ATF, Secret Service, US customs, and I believe one agent from the Coast Guard. The training consisted primarily of classroom instruction with weekly firearms instruction and qualifications in the basement of the U.S. Treasury building. Areas covered included federal laws as it related to treasury enforcement, interviewing, photography, effective writing, processing defendants, raid planning, obtaining and execution of a search warrant, arrest techniques, and testifying in court.

I learned that a lot of case law relating to search and seizure, as well as conspiracy resulted from ATF liquor cases. We were initially housed in a downtown Washington hotel, but a group of us found an apartment to share in Alexandria, Virginia. I recall my roommates were Dennis Cooper and Ed Armstrong from Alabama, Jack Batts from Tennessee and Bud Bleyman from Buffalo, New York. The school lasted from September 23rd to November 5th, at which time I returned to my Raleigh office.

In January 1970, I returned to the Washington DC area for ATF Basic Investigator School, which was held in an office building in Alexandria, Virginia. The same group of us again roomed together in the apartments in Alexandria. This school lasted only four weeks and consisted of ATF investigators only, and instruction was in ATF laws, jurisdiction and procedures.

H.T. Bracey, a supervisor in Charleston I believe, was the class coordinator and lead instructor. Plessy Williams, one of ATF's first black investigators, taught a block on undercover operations. He told of some of his experiences in working undercover, and those of Phil McGuire, who he described as ATF's best undercover man. The school focused on all aspects of ATF laws and investigative procedures, but as I recall more on firearms than liquor. The Gun Control Act of 1968 had just been enacted, and some of the powers-to-be had figured out that firearms enforcement would be ATF's future rather than moonshine whiskey. It was fortunate that some recognized that firearms enforcement was the future for ATF, because I don't think most in the Southeast ever envisioned the end of moonshining. Most would have been perfectly content to keep working the moonshiners and stills until they were no more.

Chapter Two
THE SOUTHEAST REGION

W hat is now the Bureau of Alcohol, Tobacco, Firearms and Explosives (ATF), an agency of the U.S. Justice Department, was in 1969 a division of the Internal Revenue Service, U.S. Treasury Department. The primary function of the ATFD was to enforce the federal alcohol laws and to regulate and tax the liquor and tobacco industries. The IRS was set up and functioned as seven independent regions: Southeast in Atlanta, Mid-Atlantic in Philadelphia, North-Atlantic in New York, Central in Cincinnati, Midwest in Chicago, Southwest in Dallas, and Western in San Francisco.

Each IRS region was directed by a Regional Commissioner, and an Assistant Regional Commissioner (ARC) was in charge of the ATFD. The Southeast Region, headquartered in Atlanta, was responsible for enforcement and compliance operations in seven southeast states — North Carolina, South Carolina, Georgia, Alabama, Tennessee, Mississippi, and Florida.

Under the Regional office were the District Offices for criminal enforcement and Area Offices for compliance operations. As far as criminal enforcement, each of the seven states was a District with a Special Investigator in Charge (SIC) and an Assistant Special Investigator in Charge (ASIC). Within the districts there were field offices known as posts of duty (POD), each with an Investigator in Charge (IC) and assigned Special Investigators (SI). Somewhat unique and short-lived was the position of Area Supervisor (not to be confused with Area Supervisor position in Regulatory). The Area Supervisor was over two or more PODs. I did not understand then, and have not figured out since, just exactly what the Area Supervisor's role and responsibilities were. Someone, Fulton Dukes as I recall, said their only job was to get the tires and antifreeze for the government cars from the district office (for some unknown reason back then you could not purchase tires and antifreeze directly from a local retailer), and to make sure there were sufficient beverages on hand at conferences, meetings, and other special occasions.

The Assistant Regional Commissioner for the Southeast Region was William N. "Bill" Griffin, a giant of a man in physical stature as well as power and influence. Mr. Griffin, I heard, had played professional football prior to his government service. He was a god-like figure and revered by many, a little less so to a few, but feared by most all. Perhaps not a complete authoritarian as described by the few, there was little doubt that he was in charge and most all policy decisions were made by him or certainly went through him for final approval. It was said that many personnel actions (assignments, transfers, disciplinary actions) were sometimes made over a cup of coffee or perhaps something a little stronger. His hands-on management was good in that personnel and policy decisions could be made and implemented without all the bureaucratic strings, haggling and delays that came later. On the other hand, it could be bad if you and your boss didn't get along and he had the ARC's ear. My characterization of Mr. Griffin was pretty much based on comments of the old-timers, although I did meet him a couple times later on. His appearance, demeanor and actions in those brief meetings did not change my assessment and perception that he was indeed the man in charge.

The Charlotte or North Carolina District, as it was sometimes called, was headed by the SIC Jarvis Brewer, and ASIC John Wurtele. There were seventeen PODs in the Charlotte District: Asheville, Bryson City, Charlotte, Dunn, Elizabeth City, Fayetteville, Goldsboro, Greensboro, Hickory, New Bern, Raleigh, Rocky Mount, Salisbury, Wilkesboro, Williamston, Wilmington, and Winston-Salem. Each POD was led by an Investigator in Charge and had varying numbers of Special Investigators assigned.

Most of the illicit liquor activity (making and selling moonshine) was occurring in the seven Southeast states—North Carolina, South Carolina, Tennessee, Georgia, Alabama, Mississippi, and Tennessee. In 1969 there were 9,647 stills seized in the U.S. by local, state and federal law enforcement officers. Of that total, 8,941 or 92.7% were seized in the Southeast Region. A substantial part of the moonshine was consumed within the region, but a lot was exported to other areas of the country.

Moonshine making and consumption in the Southeast was due to several factors, but really boiled down to two, the first being the availability, or unavailability I should say, of legal liquor. A majority of the counties and cities in the southeast were dry—that is, there were no legal liquor outlets. The second reason was that moonshine whiskey was cheaper to buy than legal liquor. For example, if you lived in a dry county you might have to drive an hour or two to the closest liquor store and pay $15 to $18 for a half gallon. Or, you could drive ten minutes to the local bootlegger and buy a half-gallon for $5.

Still seizures in the US peaked in 1956 when 25,608 stills were seized by federal, state, and local officers. By 1969 that number had decreased to 9,647 or by 62.3%. The decrease was due to several factors. Legal liquor became more available as the Legal Liquor Industry campaigned and pushed for more counties to go wet, and they did. Every gallon of moonshine sold meant a gallon of legal liquor not sold and the taxes not collected. Also, the federal government stepped up its enforcement activities with "Operation Dry Up" programs throughout the region. Operation Dry Up included a public awareness program, as well as stepped up enforcement. Signs, posters, fans, rulers, and other anti-moonshine items were distributed to churches, schools, businesses and other places. Its purpose was to make the public aware of the (alleged) dangers of drinking moonshine, and to encourage citizens to report to law enforcement any suspicious activities. And the death nail came when the price of sugar quadrupled and sent the price of moonshine up to the point it cost nearly as much as legal liquor. Though the seizures were declining, there was still a lot of moonshine being made in the Southeast.

Thusly, most of the ATF enforcement activity and many of the investigators were assigned to the seven Southeastern states. We knew or suspected there were other ATFD investigators throughout the country, but had very little contact or interaction with them. I do recall early on meeting two investigators from South Hill and one from Richmond on a few occasions (Southern and Southwestern Virginia had a lot of moonshining activity).

As far as those in the Southeast Region were concerned the Southeast Region was ATF, Atlanta was the headquarters, Bill Griffin was the man in charge, and our job was catching the moonshiners and bootleggers. Certainly most, if not all, were aware of that new gun law that had passed the previous year (The Gun Control Act of 1968), but we knew (and were told) our primary job was working liquor, and we would just do that "gun stuff" when we had a little extra time. That would change dramatically in a few short years as Atlanta would again fall as the term "Think Nationally" and "One Bureau" was starting to be said.

The Raleigh office (and the North Carolina District to a lesser extent) was in the process of a buildup in staffing. This buildup was a result of estimates of the illicit liquor activity in the Raleigh area, and the staff needed to address the problem. The estimates of activity and the needed buildup in staffing were probably overstated. In North Carolina alone, still seizures had declined 46% just in the previous four years from 2589 in 1966 to 1405 in 1969. But there was still a lot of moonshine activity in the Raleigh POD area. In fact, five of the major violators on the North Carolina Top Twenty Major Violator List lived and operated in the Raleigh POD area. Additionally, three major violators on the list operated in the adjoining Dunn and Rocky Mount POD areas.

The January 1971 Southeast Region Illicit Distillery Survey Estimates (also known as ATLIDS for Atlanta Illicit Distillery Survey, an estimate of active moonshine stills in a county) for Franklin County showed thirteen stills with a total mash capacity of 49,200 gallons. Although Franklin County was the most prolific for liquor activity, there were seven other counties in the Raleigh POD area: Wake, Durham, Orange, Granville, Person, Vance, and Warren. To a lesser extent, there was moonshining activity in all the counties. In the Dunn POD area, Johnston County in particular, there was significant moonshining activity with two Major Violators operating in the area.

While the primary and stated justification for the increased manpower was the estimate of liquor activity, I am sure the new firearms law was a factor also. And as it turned out, in a relatively short period the firearms laws and later explosives laws became the justification for sustaining the staffing level. Before the Raleigh buildup was completed in the early 1970s, five additional investigators were assigned to Raleigh. Veteran investigators Bill Maine,

Joe Kopka, and Chuck Stanfill transferred in from Georgia, John Spidell transferred over from the Border Patrol, and new investigators Stanley Burroughs and Gene Calcote reported. Brawley later transferred to the US Secret Service and Burroughs to the Bureau of Narcotics and Dangerous Drugs (now DEA).

So, that was the setting (of course being a new guy I was pretty much oblivious to the situation and dynamics at the time) as I was just starting out my new job as a GS-5 criminal investigator (Special Investigator) with the ATFD, often referred to then as the ATU (Alcohol Tax Unit). All I knew and cared about was that they gave me a badge, gun, handcuffs, and a car (pickup truck), and said, "Go out there and catch them moonshiners." And they were going to pay me, too — $7,720 per year, which included $6,176.00 base pay plus $1,544.00 AUO (administrative uncontrollable overtime).

Chapter Three

MOONSHINE LIQUOR (WHAT, WHERE, HOW)

Moonshine liquor (white lightening, rot-gut, mountain dew, hooch, corn liquor, non-tax-paid liquor, bootleg liquor, illicit whiskey) is distilled alcohol and has been made in the Southeastern United States for decades. It is illegal because the moonshiner does not register his still with or obtain a permit from the federal government, and more importantly, does not pay the taxes on the moonshine produced. The term "moonshine" is derived from the fact that most stills were located in woods and run at night by the light of the moon to avoid detection. The moonshiner makes the liquor and the bootlegger distributes and sells the liquor, but the terms are often used interchangeably to mean the same.

Making moonshine, some say, is an art and they claim to have special recipes and secret ingredients to make theirs better than the rest. I have tasted a lot of moonshine liquor and it is certainly true that some were a little smoother than others, but I can't really say any tasted good. Well, let me reconsider that. I do recall some "real apple brandy" we purchased undercover in Orange County (brandy supposedly came from Wilkes County). Having had some experience and being the POD unofficial taster, I took a few sips and I must say that the "Wilkes County brandy" was quite smooth and mellow.

Secret recipes and methods not withstanding, making moonshine for the most part is pretty simple. You mix water, sugar, yeast, and perhaps a little corn or some other type meal and after a few days depending on the mixture and temperature, the mixture (mash) ferments. When the mash "is right" you add a heat source and cook the mash to approximately 173 degrees (the boiling point for alcohol), at which time the alcohol will boil off, changing to a vapor state. The vapors are pushed through a copper line to a condenser. The condenser contains cool water and as the vapor in the copper coil (worm) cools it returns to a liquid state and you have distilled alcohol. The basic process is the same as used by the legal liquor makers, but it becomes moonshine and illegal because Uncle Sam does not get his cut ($10.50 a gallon in 1969).

The moonshine or illicit distillery was usually located and operated in the woods, and consisted of many components—mash barrels, caps, condensers, cooler boxes, mixing barrels, thumpers, doublers, flake stands, water pumps, water hoses, sugar, jars, and, of course, the still itself. Although the still is just one of the components, the entire distillery is often referred to as "the still". There are several types of stills and configurations, but in the Raleigh area there were primarily three types of stills: the copper pot, the submarine still, and the metal tank still. The copper pot still, as the name indicates, uses a copper pot to distill the alcohol, most often heated by wood. In some cases, barrels are used to make and ferment the mash and then put in the copper pot for distillation. The copper pot still is often associated with the Snuffy Smith type moonshiner. For the most part, the copper pots stills were relatively small and used to make "drinking liquor".

The submarine still was made with woods sides and top with metal on the bottom and ends. The name is derived from its shape— it is flat on the top and rounded on the bottom and ends, which resembles the shape of a submarine when the cap is put on the still. The submarine still usually ranged in sizes from 200 gallons to 900 gallons, and often several were used at a distillery. The advantage of the sub still is that you can mix the mash in the still and when ready, cook the mash in the still without having to transfer the mash from other containers. When the mash is ready, you can simply put the cap on (often a 55-gallon barrel cut in half) and connect the flow lines and turn up the heat. I recall a few times that wood was used as the heat source, but in most cases the stills were heated by metal burners with propane gas. The burners were a length of metal pipe with slits cut along the pipe with a propane tank attached, and functioned pretty much the same as the burner in your gas grill. Propane was readily available, could be easily controlled, and eliminated a lot of hard work getting and cutting wood.

The metal tank stills or vats were made from steel usually rectangular in shape. They operated pretty much the same as the sub still (and were often referred to as subs) but in most cases were much larger and like the subs there were often several at the distillery. Subs and metal tank distilleries were usually very large consisting not only of the stills themselves but several barrels for mash. The liquor produced at these large stills was "made to sell" liquor.

A few steam stills were found in the Raleigh area, but they were much more commonplace in the mountains of Western NC. The "Wilkes County Steam Plants" as the old timers called them, were usually very large operations and as the name indicates, used a boiler and steam to cook the mash. Steam stills required a little more knowledge and expertise to operate, and it was said that "steam liquor" was better than "sub liquor."

As the demand for moonshine lessened, some of the moonshiners went in together and put up very large mega stills, with each taking a portion of the liquor made. These stills were very large metal tanks very similar to underground gas storage tanks at gas stations. They were pretty much automated and ranged in size up to 15,000 or more gallons. They were concealed in buildings or underground, and usually located in remote areas far from the violators residences sometimes even in other states.

The small copper and one or two submarine stills were usually located relatively close to the moonshiners' home or on property of a relative or one of his trusted associates. They were usually located on or near a small creek or other water source. They could sometimes be found by dropping off and walking a circle around the moonshiner's house looking for a work way to the still, either a foot path or vehicle trail. The larger stills were more often found distances away from the moonshiners' home base and were more difficult to locate. Information from informants, surveillance, and undercover investigations were often used to locate the larger stills.

Once located, officers raided the still with the goal to catch and arrest the moonshiners and to seize and destroy the still, moonshine, and related materials. In most cases, the still was watched by officers for varying periods of time to determine who comes and goes and when the moonshiners are going to run the still. Raiding a still located within a building was usually accomplished by obtaining and executing a search warrant for the premises. Exits were covered and the executing officers went in and apprehend and arrest those inside.

Raiding a still in the woods was a pretty simple procedure with the goal, of course, of catching all the moonshiners in the act. Typically, officers were concealed in strategic locations in the woods around the still. The number of officers needed varied depending on the size of the still, its locations, and the number of still hands expected to be present at the time of the raid. It was a good idea to have at least as many officers as there were moonshiners.

Usually, one officer positioned himself near the work way (foot or vehicle access trail) so as to be able to see or hear the violators arrive. He was known as the flush man and officers surrounding the still were the catchers. At the opportune time the flush man maneuvered close to the still with the expectation of catching one moonshiner before being seen, and he then alerted the other officers whose job was to run down and catch the other fleeing moonshiners.

Some officers were better still raiders than others. They seemed to be able to sense exactly where to be to catch the fleeing moonshiners, and of course being a fast runner was helpful. ATF agent Mike Zetts, Wake ABC Officer Buzzy Anthony and Johnston ABC Officer Guy Lee were very good still raiders. I witnessed Guy Lee catch three fleeing still hands at one still, and I am told ATF Agent Carl Bowers accomplished the same feat on one occasion.

After the raid, the still and all its components had to be inventoried and destroyed, as well as any moonshine or raw materials found. In the case of the small copper pots and small subs that could usually be accomplished by chopping with an axe. The metal vats and large subs stills (often with many mash barrels) were usually destroyed by explosives. Each agent carried a case or two of dynamite or TNT blocks and some military composition C-4 and a roll of safety fuse in the trunk of his car, and a box of blasting caps in the glove compartment. Charges were made by cutting varying lengths of fuse, placing a cap one end of the fuse, and inserting the fused cap into the dynamite or TNT. The other end of the fuse would be slit open to expose the powder trail. Then depending on the number needed, agents with multiple charges would stand in a circle, light one of the fuses and all the others would then in turn light theirs off that one. Once all were lit (which sometimes was problematic), the agents would drop one in each of the barrels or stills assigned to him. Then it was "fire in the hole" and you took off for cover to await and count the charges as they went off.

Sometimes, all did not go off and you had to find the one or ones that did not detonate and recharge them. This could present a delicate and dangerous situation and as the ATF Training Manual said, "should be handled by persons thoroughly trained and experienced in the use of explosives." In reality, however, the task was often assigned to the young, inexperienced agent trainee. I recall early on helping Dunn agents raid a still in Johnston County, and when one of the charges did not go off being told by Investigator in Charge Bob Furr to "Go in there, boy, and check it out." As I neared (very slowly), the fuse all of sudden started smoking and burning and I got the hell out of there before it detonated.

The use of explosives to destroy stills was probably one of the most dangerous parts of the job. Raleigh agents Bill Walden and Bill Maine, both experienced investigators, were injured when a number of blasting caps exploded as they were preparing charges to blow up a still in Vance County. The danger was lessened considerably when we started using detonating cord (det-cord) and later on binary explosives. The det-cord was itself an explosive and you could connect any number of charges to it and when it ignited all the charges ignited simultaneously. The binary or Kinepack explosives were in the form of a powder and a liquid and only when mixed together become an explosive.

The large stills in buildings or underground often had to be removed from the building or underground site to be destroyed. Some of the larger ones actually had to be disassembled and cut up with a torch and removed with a crane. On one occasion, Agent Devaney and I located a metal tank still under an abandoned house in Franklin County, and although it was relatively small it was too big to take out through the basement door. So, we decided to make and place a C-4 shape charge on top of the still with the idea that the charge would explode downward, cutting a hole in the top and bottom of the still. And we did and when it went off, it appeared the house raised off its foundation. We assumed the still was destroyed and decided to take our leave.

Chapter Four

MOONSHINE ALL AROUND
(1970)

M y training over, I was ready to get in the field and start to work. As is the case with all new agents, I was assigned a training officer to look after me and train me during my probationary year. It was pointed out that during that probationary year you could be terminated for any reason—or for no reason—and if you were smart (and I was) you'll just keep your mouth shut, do what you were told, and don't ask too many questions. Seasoned investigators who had been on the job for years didn't care too much about your opinions or new ideas on how things should be done. Tommy Stokes was my primary training officer and he taught me a great deal about liquor enforcement as well as report writing. Someone once said, "It ain't necessarily what you do but what your report said you did," which I found to be often the case over the years. Tommy was assigned Franklin County, and as his trainee I, too, worked a great deal in Franklin County.

My First Moonshine

The first month out of school, we found and seized five stills and two loads of liquor—three stills in Franklin County and one each in Johnston and Vance counties. The liquor seizures were both in Franklin County, the largest being 90 gallons near Youngsville.

One of the Franklin County stills was a 900-gallon submarine behind a juke joint on NC-56 west of Franklinton. After a couple days of surveillance, we arrested Herman "Bro" Harris when he came to run the still. The still, along with 800 gallons of mash and six gallons of non-tax-paid liquor (NTPW) was seized and destroyed. I remember distinctly how cold it was the two nights we laid on the snow and ice-covered ground. We had very warm sleeping bags that we had obtained from the Army surplus, and I remember commenting to Mr. Zetts (Mike) about the sleeping bags and he informed me that they were "observation bags"—not sleeping bags! There would be many more cold and wet days and nights, but it didn't matter because I loved what I was doing.

A few months later, we received information that Harris had a still in an outbuilding behind his house. A search warrant was obtained and executed at his residence in Franklinton. The search resulted in the discovery and seizure of three sub stills, 1,300 gallons of mash and forty-eight gallons of moonshine. We also found several containers of rubbing alcohol that were being used to "spike" the moonshine. Harris was again arrested on state charges.

In keeping with the policy that small stills and liquor cases would be tried in State court and more significant stills would be tried in Federal court, the cases were tried in Franklin County District Court. Mike and Franklin County Sheriff William Dement had an understanding about working liquor in the county. Any liquor information that the Sheriff received (and he got a lot), he would pass on to Mike to check out and investigate. In return, Mike would call the Sherriff when seizures and arrests were made so the Sheriff could get his picture in the paper (he was a politician and an elected official) and confiscate the copper, gas tanks, and other materials from the destroyed still to sell for county school funding. The arrangement was beneficial to the Sheriff and to us as well. The Sheriff had only four uniformed deputies for the whole county: Chief Deputy David Batton in Bunn, John Deal in Franklinton, Leroy Terrell in Ingleside, and Lloyd Gupton in Centerville. With only those four deputies and no investigators, he had very little ability to investigate all the tips and information he got, but under our arrangement he got the credit (in the paper) and the booty from the still. ATF, on the other hand, received a lot of liquor information from the sheriff (probably fifty percent or more) that resulted in seizures and arrests that were reported as stats for the Raleigh office.

And My Damn Handcuffs, Too

In March, Mike received information that violator Verris Cooper was operating a small still near his home in the Pilot section of Franklin County. He enlisted Don (Devaney) to drive him there and drop him off to check out the area. Mike found the small submarine still and observed two men working in and about the distillery. While perhaps the prudent thing to do would have been to withdraw and return with Don, Mike (not surprisingly) decided to raid the still by himself. He caught one man, but the second man ran away. Mike handcuffed the captured man to a small tree and gave chase after the fleeing moonshiner. After a futile chase, Mike returned to the still yard and, to his surprise, the captured man and "his handcuffs" were nowhere to be found. Mike was a proud, confidant, no nonsense man, and not someone who took well to being embarrassed or made to look foolish. He immediately went to Cooper's house and informed him that it would be best if the two escapees and his "damn handcuffs, too" would be at the Franklin County Courthouse the following morning. Mr. Cooper took his advice and did appear the following morning with the handcuffs and identified the still hands as being his brother and son, both of whom were arrested and convicted in state court.

The "Revenuer Loses Handcuffs" story wound up in *The Franklin Times*, and other than Mike and the Coopers, most found the whole episode to be quite humorous. It was puzzling as to who might have reported the story to the *Times*: Mike certainly would not have, and Don steadfastly denied reporting the story to the newspaper. The puzzle was solved when it was later noted that *The Franklin Times* story cited *The Durham Morning Herald* as the source of the story. It had to be Don. He had first-hand details of the incident, Durham was his assigned territory, and he had the contacts at the newspaper. I'm not sure the ruse fooled Mike, but I suppose Don could in good conscience continue to deny giving the story to *The Franklin Times*.

1001 Gallons of Moonshine

In April, information was received that major violator Lonless Fields had a large cache of moonshine in a tobacco barn located on the premises of Russell Evans near Creedmoor. Along with Granville County ABC Chief Arthur Ray Currin and Wake County ABC officers Buzzy Anthony and Bill Sparkman, we conducted surveillance at the property. After seeing no activity for several days, we obtained and subsequently executed a search warrant at the property. We found and seized 1,001 gallons of moonshine in the barn contained in half-gallon glass jars and one-gallon plastic jugs. The two types of containers were reflective of when the moonshiners began changing from glass jars to plastic jugs. The illicit liquor was destroyed, and Evans was arrested. No evidence was found linking Fields to the liquor.

UDS Seizures

In April, Investigator Devaney and I located a small sub still near Wake X Roads in Wake County. The still was not set up and appeared to be abandoned, so we decided to seize and destroy it and write it up as a UDS (Unknown Defendant Seizure). A UDS report signifies a seizure with no arrest or known defendant. You really didn't want to have too many "no arrest or known defendant" seizures. As both Raleigh and Wake counties became more populated and urbanized in the late '60s and early '70s, moonshiners pretty much moved out to the more rural areas in neighboring Franklin and Granville counties. However, I do remember finding and seizing a few stills in the Raleigh area. We seized two subs underground where the Leesville School now stands, two small stills near the Mount Vernon Church, one on Durant Road, and one in a house on Capital Blvd where the Triangle Shopping Center is now located.

They All Got Away

In May, information was received that major violator Louis Dorsey had a large still in the Centerville area of Franklin County. Mike, Tommy (Stokes) and I found the distillery deep in the woods a few miles from Centerville. It was a large still consisting of eight 1,125-gallon steel vats and two 940-gallon steel vats with approximately 8,000 gallons of mash. While checking the area, we observed a car going very slowly along the road with Tony Dorsey, the son of Louis Dorsey, riding on the fender looking around, apparently checking for any signs of law enforcement. Because of the size of the distillery, the powers-to-be (Mike and DC) decided it would serve as a textbook training case for new investigators and a model of how to work a still completely. Rather than just raid the still and catch the still hands, we would conduct an around-the-clock surveillance to not only identify those operating the still, but to follow the liquor to see where it was going, identify the source of the raw materials, and hopefully identify the owners of the still.

Two teams were set up with the plan that one would work the on-the-ground surveillance and the other to work activity to and from the still. Stokes and Walden were the two team leaders, with Stokes' team being the ground team. We had activity in and around the still the first two days and nights, but the ATF plane was unable to assist due to weather.

On the third day, the teams were to switch assignments. Stokes and Walden were good friends but were also very competitive, occasionally trying to outdo each other. So, given the weather and inability to conduct aerial surveillance, the decision was made that we should go ahead and raid the still the following morning; that way, both teams would be involved in the raid and arrest, and neither would feel out-done by the other. Walden's team was dropped off and we all surrounded the still to await the violators. Regional Investigator Joe Carter was working the case, as Louis Dorsey was one of his major violators and the sighting of his son was evidence that Dorsey owned the still or certainly had a hand in it to some extent. The raid plan was that Joe would take a position along the still path a few hundred yards from the still, radio when the still hands approached, and then flush the still.

Shortly after getting into position, the sound of a vehicle approaching could be heard in the distance. A few minutes later, sounds could be heard, and movement observed in and about the still area. They were in there and the adrenalin began to build as we waited for the still hands to settle into their work. Five or ten minutes passed and nothing could be seen or heard in or about the still. Then, another few minutes passed and nothing was heard. Something obviously was not right and we all cautiously moved up to the still and discovered there was no one there. A few minutes later, Joe came walking down the still path and asked what had happened. We told him that someone had come to the still, started to work, and apparently saw something that spooked him and left. Joe insisted that he had not seen anyone come by him to or from the still.

Of course, the speculation and blame ensued but the bottom line was "they all got away"—or did they? Before blowing up the still, we were able to lift some latent fingerprints off some of the still equipment. The latent fingerprints were sent to the Atlanta lab, where they were identified as being the fingerprints of Tony Mitchell Sidden, a Wilkes County moonshiner with prior moonshining convictions. Sidden was located and arrested and set for trial in Franklin County District court.

In most liquor cases tried in State court, the charges were misdemeanors and tried initially in the District court. The routine would be that the defendant would plead guilty in District court and be fined and given a suspended sentence. If the fine was too high or in the rare occasion an active sentence was imposed, the defendant would simply appeal the case to Superior court and demand a jury trial, knowing that the sentence would probably be reduced to avoid the time and cost of a jury trial. Sidden was already on federal probation and knew if he pled guilty or was found guilty in District court his federal probation would be revoked and he would be off to prison. So, he (or someone) hired one of the top lawyers in Franklin County and asked for a jury trial in Superior Court.

The State's case was the testimony of two officers who identified Sidden as the man they had seen working in and around the still during the surveillance, and his fingerprints were found at the still. The defendant's case, truly unique and simple, was that the **IRS Revenuers** were not playing the game fair. That if the defendant was running the still they had ample opportunity to arrest him but did not, and now to save face they were trying to convict him with the so-called latent fingerprints and questionable identification of the embarrassed officers. He summed up his case by telling the jurors that here you have all these **IRS Revenuers and Tax Collectors** with all the resources of the **federal Internal Revenue Service** coming in from **Washington, DC** to our little Franklin County and trying to railroad one of our poor little citizens on trumped up charges. He closed by again saying that if the defendant was operating the still they should have laid hands on him and arrested him there, but they did not and now should not be allowed to convict the defendant just to save face and avoid the embarrassment.

"Are you going to allow these **IRS Revenuers and Tax Agents** to do this?" he asked. The jury said, "No, we are not" and found Sidden not guilty. So, they did all get away. But for Sidden, a guilty verdict and long prison sentence might have saved him from his current situation, where he sits on Death Row in Central Prison in Raleigh awaiting execution (2020).

According to published reports and court records, Sidden and his stepson, Anthony Blankenship, murdered Gary Sidden during a robbery in Yadkin County in 1982. They also kidnapped his two sons, who had witnessed the robbery and murder, and later shot each in the back of the head and threw their bodies in an old well. They were convicted of the robbery and murder of the father in 1984 and sentenced to life terms. At that time it was not known that the boys were dead, they were just considered missing persons. In 1991, Blankenship, while in prison, confessed that he and Sidden had kidnapped and murdered the two boys and led officers to where they had thrown the bodies. They were subsequently tried and convicted of kidnapping and murder. Sidden received the death penalty and has been on death row since 1995. No execution date has been set as he continues to appeal his conviction and sentence.

The Militant File

Early on Mike assigned me to work with Investigator Bobby Sherrill, who was working on an investigation of "militant activity" in Durham. The investigation surrounded the activity of Howard Fuller and other so-called militants who were supposedly establishing a Malcolm X University in Durham. It was all "hush hush" stuff according to Bobby, and no one else at the POD was to know about it.

The investigation pretty much consisted of him going through newspapers and circling in red any articles or references to the militants' names and activities. And yes, this is where I came in, as my assignment was to take my government issued scissors and cut out the circled articles and place them in the "Militant File". He, or the Durham PD, did have one informant that he was paying on a regular basis for information about the "militant activity".

While I only met the informer on a couple occasions, it was my impression that the informer was in it for the money and never provided any useful information. Whether Bobby opened the investigation on his own or it was assigned to him out of the District Office I never knew. But when Leonard Mika became SIC and became aware of the investigation, he ordered it stopped immediately and any and all militant files destroyed. It was a bitter setback for Bobby, but a great relief for me that I could get back to work in Franklin County.

The Oxford Firebombings

In May 1970, civil unrest and violence in the form of firebombings erupted in Oxford, North Carolina. We were asked to assist local and state officers in attempting to suppress the violence and apprehend those causing the problems. The city of Oxford was put under curfew, which was enforced by the local police, Sheriff's Department, SBI, and Highway Patrol. Together, we attempted to suppress the firebombings, which lasted two or three evenings. We arrested six individuals and seized a number of firebombs (Molotov cocktails). The individuals arrested were all young, with three not even 16 years old. While these youngsters were apprehended for carrying, and in some cases throwing the firebombs, local officials blamed local civil rights activists, including Ben Chavis, for the outbreak of fires and violence. I do not know and have no personal knowledge that Chavis or any of the local leaders were involved, and there was no evidence linking any of them to the firebombings. Chavis and some of his associates were later charged and convicted in a firebombing in Wilmington, North Carolina. The convictions were subsequently overturned and just recently the so-called "Wilmington 10" were pardoned by the outgoing governor of North Carolina.

Douglas Freeman Ross

Doug Ross was repudiated to be one of the most prolific "liquor men" in the state. He lived and operated out of the Pines (his house, café, and mobile home park) on US 1 north of Franklinton. He was listed at or near the top of the Top Twenty North Carolina Major Violator List with an estimated weekly distribution of 2400 gallons of liquor. He was number one on the Franklin County ATLIDS with an estimated distilling capacity of 15,000 gallon of mash. Ross was arrested and convicted of conspiracy in connection with a large still seized in Yadkin County in

1969. He continued to operate at full speed while awaiting trial and during his appeal after the conviction. During that period, we continued to investigate and conduct surveillance at the Pines and elsewhere. We located a couple of liquor stashes as a result of the surveillance at the Pines.

In July, we were able to follow a car from the Pines to a remote house located on Hwy 56 west of Franklinton just inside Granville County. SI Stokes, Calcote and I dropped off and set up surveillance in the woods near the house. It was hot and raining when we went in and neither let up for two days and nights. Brushing against the wet foliage as we went in, we all were infested with chiggers or as we call them red bugs. As you can imagine, it was a long and unpleasant two days and nights. And, to make thing worse, we were not even sure there was any liquor in the outbuilding behind the house. There were two large dogs on the property, and each time we tried to approach the outbuilding they would alert, start barking, and look for us. Normally, if circumstances allow, you find a way to look in the suspected stash before spending two or three days on surveillance. In this case, all we could do was to wait and see. Thanks to Calcote, we did have plenty to eat. Most investigators when going in the woods take a little something to eat: a pack of crackers, a can of beanie-weenies, a candy bar, etc. Well, Calcote took a whole cardboard box of eats in including fried chicken and biscuits and was kind enough to share (sparingly and begrudgingly).

On the third day as we were breaking camp and getting ready to leave, a pickup truck with a large camper shell turned off the highway, slowly came up the dirt driveway and backed up to the small outbuilding at the rear of the house. A car followed onto the driveway and to the house a few minutes later. Suddenly there was no more heat, no more rain, and no more red bugs. We watched as the drivers of the truck and car, along with a man from the house, started to unload something from the truck into the outbuilding. We moved up cautiously and, after observing that it was gallon plastic jugs, moved in. I grabbed the old man from the house, Tommy caught the truck driver, but the driver of the car took off and out-ran us all. However, we recognized him as being Johnny Henry Branch, one of Doug's drivers, and later arrested him at his house. We seized the truck and the 674 gallons of moonshine being delivered.

Branch denied that he was the man unloading the liquor and pleaded not guilty in Granville County Court. The trial was held before Judge Linwood Peoples and as the first witness (Calcote) took the stand to identify Branch, a deputy approached and had a side bar conversation with the Judge. Afterwards, Judge Peoples asked the defendant if he was in fact Johnny Henry Branch, at which time the defendant remained silent and looked at his attorney. Judge Peoples addressed the defendant and his attorney and said he was calling a ten minute recess and when the court re-convened, the defendant "John Henry Branch" had better be the one in the defendant's chair or someone or *someones* would be going to jail for contempt of court. As it turns out, John Henry Branch had a twin brother and it was the twin in the defendant's chair. The plan was that the twin would be identified as the fleeing bootlegger (and he would have as they were identical) and after divulging that he was not John Henry Branch the case would be dismissed. When court re-convened the attorney apologized to the court and denied any involvement in or knowledge of the attempted ruse.

On a lighter note, we were conducting a lengthy surveillance of the Pines from a wooded area across the road (US 1). One particular night Don and Bill Walden were on the ground surveillance and reported to Mike the following morning that everything was quiet and no activity was observed during the night. Mike asked them if they were sure and they assured him there was no activity and all was quiet the entire night. Mike informed them there had been an attempted break-in at the restaurant around midnight and officers from the Franklinton Police, Sheriff's Department, and the Highway Patrol had responded to and remained at the scene for some time conducting their investigation. Don and Bill could not understand how they could have missed it all. Mike and everyone else knew exactly what happened!

We continued to investigate Ross until he went off to prison. After serving his sentence, Doug, like many other old bootleggers, turned to dealing drugs as the moonshine business continued to decline. Most turned to growing and disturbing marijuana, I think partly because they could rationalize that, like liquor, it really was not that bad. Doug however, got involved in the hard stuff and was subsequently investigated and indicted by the FBI for cocaine trafficking in the 1980s. And we (ATF) had not heard the last of Doug Ross either. We would cross paths again and for Doug things did not end well at all.

Sources of Information

To be successful in working liquor, as in most law enforcement, you rely heavily on information. That information comes in many forms and from many sources, including: good citizens, wives and girlfriends, neighbors, rivals and competitors. Some become informants for personal reasons and don't expect payment for their information, and others are semi-professional informants who expect to be paid for the information. Most all, including the semi-professional informants, want only to pass along the information anonymously, and never testify in court.

Sometimes a still hand or small-time violator caught with a small amount of liquor would give information on his boss, supplier or a competitor in exchange for leniency in his own case. For example: you catch Joe, a small-time retailer with 30 or 40 gallons of liquor, and you ask him to identify his supplier. As an incentive to cooperate, you might offer options in his case in exchange for assistance in naming and catching his supplier. His options might be (A) put his case in federal court where he will certainly get a prison sentence, or (B) going to state court where he will probably be fined, or (C) even the possibility that he may not be charged at all and it will all just go away (legal authority questionable but occasionally exercised).

A few flat out refused to help and took option A, some took option B and gave you as little information as possible, and sometimes one would take option C and tell you everything he knew and go to work as a confidential informant. I had one such informant who had been a major violator in the past and knew about everyone in the liquor business. He would call me and say I think Doug has a stash in a tobacco barn on his farm or he would say Doug has 600 gallons stashed in a tobacco barn at his farm. The latter statement meaning he had seen it himself and most probably helped put it there.

While a necessary evil in the law enforcement business, informants often proved very difficult to work with and manage. While you were working them, some were trying to work you to their advantage, usually for more money or perhaps for you to look the other way when they were making or selling a little on the side. They could be difficult to get up with and didn't always follow instructions. A case in point, one of my best informants set up a deal to deliver a truck load of plastic jugs to a "big liquor man" in Wilkes County. He was to drive the truck to a truck stop in Yadkinville, where he would be met by someone who would take the truck, unload the jugs and return the truck to him.

I instructed him to arrive at the truck stop at exactly 1:00 pm. We set up surveillance inside and outside the truck stop and had the ATF plane in the air with the plan of course to follow the truck when it left. At 1:00 pm no Ryder truck, at 2:00 pm no Ryder truck and so on until we decided he was not coming and called off the surveillance. I tried to contact him by phone and went to his house with no luck. I finally caught up with him the next day, at which time he told me what had happened. He explained that he went up the night before to see a girl he knew up there, and the next morning drove to the truck stop to eat breakfast and ran into the man he was to meet. The man saw the truck and insisted they do the deal then and they did, some three hours before he was supposed to be there.

The Preacher

Occasionally you encounter the professional informant or, as we called them, "special employees". The special employee is willing to participate in the investigation to include making undercover buys and testifying in court. In return, he is be paid a daily subsistence while he works and an award (not reward) at the end of the case, the amount being determined by how well he did and what was accomplished.

One such person was "The Preacher", who showed up at the Raleigh office in the spring of 1970 looking for work. He professed to be a preacher and an ace undercover man and boasted "I can buy liquor from anybody". He told of his work and accomplishments in making buys in other areas of the south and furnished names of officers who could verify and vouch for him. The Preacher was a well-dressed, big black man in his forties with a real gift of gab. He drove one of the big Oldsmobile 88s and had a line of BS as long as his car. Investigator Bill Walden was given the assignment to check him out and to direct and supervise him in his endeavors in the Raleigh area. After verifying some of his references, the Preacher was given the names of some known bootleggers and sent to make buys. He was pretty successful in making buys in Wake and Granville counties, primarily small buys of two or three cases at a time. He infiltrated a group in the Creedmoor area that resulted in several arrests and the seizure of several hundred gallons of moonshine.

As a result of his success and his continuous boasting that he could buy liquor from anyone, Walden decided to send him to try to make a buy from Major Violator Doug Ross in Franklinton. The Preacher went to the Pines and met with Ross with the story he was new in the area and needed a reliable source for several-case quantities of liquor. Ross talked with him, trying to feel him out, and finally said he could supply him with liquor in any quantity he wanted, but since he did not know him he would have to do a little checking. The Preacher told him that he had been getting his liquor from EP in Zebulon, but EP was just a small dealer and his prices were too high. Doug told him that he knew EP and would check his story out, and for him (the Preacher) to come back in a few days.

The Preacher returned and met with Ross a few days later, at which time Doug told him that he had talked with EP and EP said he had never heard of him. The Preacher, not missing a beat, picked up the telephone and called EP with Doug listening in to the conversation. When EP answered the Preacher jumped all over him for telling Mr. Ross he didn't know him. EP explained that he only told Ross that so he (EP) would not lose his (Preacher's) business. That was good enough for Doug, and he sold the Preacher eight cases that day. The Preacher continued dealing with Doug and we located two large stashes in the process. Sheriff Dement and I subsequently arrested Doug on state charges relative to the undercover buys, and he pled guilty with his state sentence to run concurrently with the federal sentence to be served after the appeal process was completed.

New Federal Building

In the summer, we moved from the small building on North Street into the new federal building on New Bern Avenue, now known as the Terry Sanford Building. We went from being next door to the IRS (our offices were at the rear of the building away from the visiting public) to being next door to the FBI. We are talking about the J. Edgar Hoover FBI with the white shirts, ties and jackets. I think they, like the IRS folks, were a little taken aback by our lax dress and unbefitting general appearance (we often wore woods cloths and were a little unshaven and disheveled.) Our new office space was much larger and nicer, but parking at the building was somewhat limited. There were about a dozen spaces at the side of the building close to the rear entrance and the rest were in a lot a distance away. I don't know how Mike did it, but he somehow bested the FBI and others and was able to get eight of the premier spaces for ATF parking. The coveted spaces were assigned to senior investigators and the two regional investigators. Often when not being occupied, one of us juniors would park in the spaces. On one occasion I parked in Regional Investigator Ed Grays spot, thinking he was gone for the day. Well, he apparently returned and complained to Mike to "keep that damn juvenile delinquent (me) out of his space."

As our numbers increased, we ran out of office space and Mike secured an interior room across the hall with no windows and only one door. Six of us peons were given desks in that room that we named "the snake pit". We had one telephone and one or two old manual typewriters that we shared. Image having to type a daily report with five carbon copies with the old typewriters — it was a challenge. We were finally freed from the "snake pit" when we moved to a more spacious office down on the third floor. The FBI was in need of more space and made arrangements for our new space in exchange for our old space next door to them.

As the year ended, everything was going well. We were in our new space and there was still a lot of moonshine being made. Herb Steely transferred in from Alabama as the new Area Supervisor over the Raleigh and Dunn offices. DC was removed from that position and put back as a field agent. To this day, I do not know what caused DC to lose his job and be put back in the field. I heard that it had something to do with ATF's decision to not put cases in federal court in the Eastern District of North Carolina. I heard that Leonard Mika, the new SIC who replaced Jarvis Brewer, felt like that he was given some bad information (presumably by DC and others) and that he based his decision to pull out of federal court on that information. I do not know if that was the case or not, but in any event, Herb Steely became the new Area Supervisor. Herb, like DC, was a very likable person and a good manager and supervisor. He, unlike D.C., enjoyed the woods and spent a lot of time working with the agents in the field.

Chapter Five

REVENUER VS. MOONSHINER (JOE CARTER–PERCY FLOWERS)

Joe Carter

Although Tommy Stokes was my assigned training officer, one of my first assignments was to tag along with and assist Regional Special Investigator Joe Carter. Stationed throughout the Districts, Regional Specials worked out of the Atlanta Regional Office. They were assigned to work Major Violators and special investigations in their area. They maintained open files (or jackets as they called them) on Major Violators in their area, with the intent to charge them with conspiracy when sufficient information and evidence was obtained.

Joe was putting together a conspiracy case against Major Violators Doug Ross and Millard Ashley following the seizure of a large still in Yadkin County. The conspiracy statute is often used for Major Violators and large still owners who are seldom actually caught at the still. Under the statute, a criminal conspiracy exists when two or more persons conspire and agree to violate the law and one or more of the persons commit an overt act in furtherance of the conspiracy.

In this case, Ross and Ashley agreed to set up a still and make and distribute moonshine liquor. Ashley located a good still site and made arrangements to have the stills made and Ross obtained a large quantity of barrels and had them transported to the still. The case against Ross was pretty much circumstantial as I recall: he was seen in the area of the still on a number of occasions, several barrels found at the still had been previously located near his property in Franklin County, a couple vehicles seized traced back to him or his family members, and various tidbits connecting him to the other defendants. Joe was successful in making the case (as he most always was when wanted to and tried), and all were tried and convicted in Federal court in Winston-Salem.

Joe was also doing a follow-up investigation of the attempted shooting of our investigators in Dunn. In that case, Dunn investigators had located a still and were conducting surveillance at the residence of Julius Jackson in Dunn. Jackson discovered their presence, at which time the officers attempted to arrest him. He resisted arrest and attempted to get to a knife in his pocket but was subdued by the officers. It was a very cold morning in January, and after calming down, Jackson asked them to come into his house while they were awaiting a search warrant for the property. Mrs. Jackson made coffee, after which IC Furr told Jackson to come outside with them. Jackson asked that he be allowed to speak to his daughter, who was in an adjacent bedroom. As he started toward the bedroom followed by Furr, Mrs. Jackson yelled, "He's getting his gun".

As Furr and the other officers rushed into the bedroom, Jackson was taking his .30 caliber carbine from a wall rack. Furr grabbed Jackson as he fired two shots from the carbine, barely missing Special Investigator Henry Johnson and Cumberland County ABC Officer Underwood. As Jackson continued to struggle and attempt to shoot the carbine, Johnson fired his revolver and struck Jackson in the chest. Jackson was taken to a local hospital and after recovering was tried and convicted. Jackson had a lengthy record for numerous violations of the liquor laws and assault, and Joe's investigation strongly suggested that the attempted shooting of the officers was pre-planned and not a spur-of-the moment incident. As might be expected, a flurry of memos and directives ensued on arrest techniques and procedures as well proper handling of prisoners.

Joe Carter, in looking back, was probably the last of the breed of "ATU" officers I came to hear about at the Raleigh POD, and elsewhere I suspect. They worked hard and played hard with alcohol often present in both cases. I started to hear stories about some having a few drinks in the office, wherein on a few occasions guns were drawn and shots were fired. One story told was that a visiting officer was invited to have a drink and when he declined a gun was drawn and the invitation was extended again, at which time he accepted. Another story I heard was that some investigators were in the office late in the day and having a few drinks when the janitor came to the office to clean. He was asked to leave but apparently did not quickly enough and one or more shots were fired into the ceiling to move him along a little faster. I don't know how true, or if true at all, these stories were, but it was for sure that Raleigh in the past had a reputation and was considered a prize assignment, characterized by some as "the garden spot of ATF". There was plenty of liquor work and it was a good place to live and to play.

"You want to go a dollar on a pint?" Joe asked me one day as we were leaving the office to go to Louisburg. Not knowing, but suspecting what he meant, I said yes. We stopped at a liquor store and he got a pint of whiskey, and after getting back on the road Joe took the top off and threw it out the window remarking, "We won't need that anymore!" When he wanted to be, Joe was a tenacious investigator and would do what was necessary to make his case. I am not suggesting he would do anything illegal, but often strayed a little outside established rules and procedures. I recall once he ran out of PEA money (Purchase of Evidence Account) and instead of waiting for more funds from Atlanta, he just made the buy with his own money. He once directed me to meet an informer in Franklin County and receive custody of eight cases of liquor the informer had bought from a violator. I met the informer as directed, but he gave me only four cases rather than the eight I was supposed to get. When I inquired about the other four cases, he told me that he and Joe had an arrangement that he would turn over half and keep the other half as payment for his work. I turned the four cases over to Joe to handle and write up as he deemed appropriate.

On another occasion, we were driving to Louisburg when we were passed by a car that Joe recognized as a liquor car. He pulled it over and was talking to the driver when, all of a sudden, he and the driver began shouting at each other. Joe pulled him out of the car as the shouting escalating into a brief pushing and shoving match. As things calmed down a bit, I heard Joe tell the man to get back in the car and if he ever threatened him again, he would not only lock him up for threatening/assaulting a federal officer but whip his ass in the process. It wasn't until later that I learned that the driver was actually Joe's informer, and the whole episode was staged to enhance the informer's standing and credibility with his cohorts in the car.

Joe was stationed in Wilkesboro before coming to Raleigh, and often talked about working in Wilkesboro and all the big stills and arrests there. One of his claims to fame was that he arrested NAS-CAR legend Junior Johnson at a large still that belonged to his father. According to Joe, Johnson told him that he had only come down to the still to help his daddy with a problem he was having with a boiler. Johnson was convicted and sentenced to serve three years in prison. He later received a pardon from President Ronald Reagan. In Raleigh, Joe was responsible for a number of large seizures and arrests and was the lead investigator in pursuing notorious moonshiner Joshua Percy Flowers, "King of the Moonshiners".

Joe was quite a character and the old adage "they threw away the mold when they made him" certainly applied. He developed some serious health issues and retired on disability in 1973. He returned to his native Stanley County and became very successful in business and authored two books. Joe passed away at the age of 89 on January 25, 2018, ironically the same day as I was writing these paragraphs about him. Ed Garrison and I attended his funeral in Albemarle and from comments made from family and friends, Joe didn't change a lot from the aggressive, confidant, self-assured, flamboyant man that I had known.

Joshua Percy Flowers

"Bane of Federal agents is J. Percy Flowers, philanthropist, pillar of the church and friend of politicians" was the lead line in a 1958 edition of the *Saturday Evening Post* profiling Flowers as the "King of the Moonshiners". According to the *Post*, in 1957 the Internal Revenues Service's Alcohol and Tobacco Tax Division (ATT) seized more than 42,000 gallons of bootleg whiskey in North Carolina, almost a fifth of the total seized nationally. The article continued describing Flowers as the state's No. 1 bootlegger for years of Wilders Township in Johnston County, near Raleigh, and intimate of politicians, philanthropist, and pillar of the White Oak Baptist Church. The article quoted ATF's chief of enforcement, "I know of no seizures to compare to those made on property Flowers controls". And indeed for five decades, Percy Flowers made and sold moonshine and a lot of it. He was the target of dozens of investigations by the Federal government and various state and local agencies resulting in the seizure of many large distilleries and thousands of gallons of moonshine. He was arrested and tried numerous times on federal and state charges relating to making liquor, resulting in very few convictions and only two short prison sentences.

In August of 1935, Percy and his two brothers were charged in federal court with assault and conspiracy to kill a federal ATU inspector and Wake County constable. It seems that the two officers were left to guard the cars while a large raiding party went to the vicinity of Flowers home searching for stills and liquor. The Flowers boys came upon the officers and attacked them with sticks, the butt end of a pistol and a knife. They were arrested, tried and convicted and sentenced to a short prison term. In what was described as the biggest raid in the history of Johnston County, the officers confiscated five large whiskey plants and 19,000 gallons of mash. Not to be outdone, Percy and Jimmie Flowers swore out state warrants charging the two officers with assaulting them with a deadly weapon. Those warrants were apparently never served.

In April 1951, Percy and six other defendants were found not guilty in federal court on charges of conspiracy to defraud the U.S. Government by alleged whiskey operations over an eight-year period. Of note in that case, one of the defendants acquitted was a former Alcohol Tax officer and Wake County ABC enforcement officer.

In July 1957, Flowers and seventeen others were indicted in federal court on conspiracy charges relating to the manufacturing, possession and distribution of nontaxpaid whiskey. In that investigation, ATU investigators Leonard Mika and Roy Longnecker raided a farm owned by Percy resulting in the seizure of 2,450 gallons of "premium" bootleg liquor that had been aging for six months in 49 charred oak kegs. The kegs were of 50 gallons each and had red oak chips in the liquor to give it color. According to the officers, the "premium grade" liquor would sell for double price of regular white liquor.

During the trial in federal court, Flowers threatened an ATU investigator who was a witness in the case. The ATU investigator, a black officer from Philadelphia, reported that he was reading a newspaper during a court recess when Flowers approached him. The agent said that Flowers called him "a black S.O.B., and then threatened, "If I ever catch you down here again I will fix you". When called before the judge to face contempt of court charges, Flowers stated he was so nervous he could hardly recall what he had said, but he did remember telling the agent that he was a lying s.o.b. The judge offered Percy a chance to apologize to the witness, but Percy refused. Flowers' lawyers then unsuccessfully argued that the officer had finished testifying and was no longer a witness. The judge pointed out that the officer had testified on direct but was still subject to cross-examination and was still a witness. The judge found him guilty of contempt of court and sentenced him to 18 months in the Federal penitentiary in Atlanta. The judge later reduced the sentence to a year and a day.

In addition to his federal conviction, things were not going well for Percy at the state and local level. The Percy Flowers Store was padlocked after a state judge held that the store was being used and maintained for the purpose of carrying on his unlawful whiskey activities. He further held that Flowers was operating the business as to render and constitute the same as a public nuisance in violation of state law. At about the same time, Flowers was convicted on State liquor charges and sentenced to five years probation. While he was a pillar in the community and a large contributor to his own church, others in the nearby township were not so captivated and tolerant of his moonshining enterprises. Members of the Thanksgiving Baptist Church in nearby O'Neal Township passed a resolution condemning him and his unlawful activities and improper practices. The resolution, passed without a dissenting vote, went on to ask the public to assist law enforcement in gaining evidence to help clean up the degrading situation existing in their community.

In August 1965, Flowers was again in Federal court facing trial for conspiracy to violate the IRS liquor laws. The case hinged to a large extent on the testimony of a former tenant who testified he lived on Percy's farm and worked for him at several large moonshine stills. Special Investigator Joe Carter, out of the Raleigh office, initiated the case and supervised the former tenant, turned undercover man, in making tape recordings of his conversations with Percy in regard to liquor transactions. He was acquitted on some of the charges, and the remaining charges were dismissed by the Judge after the jury could not reach a verdict. In that case, there was testimony that Flowers inquired about Joe Carter's financial situation and asked someone if he thought Carter could use a little extra money. He was not charged relative to the inquiry, but was back in Federal court on bribery charges in 1968 and was again acquitted.

As the decade of the 60s came to an end, the era of the big-time moonshiners, too, was in decline and in a few short years would for the most part be over. Percy was still listed on the Major Violator List at number seven statewide with an estimated weekly volume of 2,000 gallons. While I suspect that the estimate was a little high (as was all the list), Percy was no doubt still in the moonshine business. In 1970, I assisted Dunn agents in the seizure of two stills on his property and the seizure of 42 gallons of moonshine near his dog lot. No one was arrested or charged in either of the seizures.

In the fall of 1970, Joe Carter, who had pursued Percy for years, initiated an undercover investigation utilizing The Preacher to attempt to buy from Percy. The Preacher was able to make buys from Percy's underlings at Flowers Stores. As a result of the buys, a search warrant was executed at Flowers Store in December that resulted in the seizure of 133 gallons of moonshine and a truck. The case was eventually tried in Johnston County court because a feud between ATF and the U.S. Attorney's Office had resulted in ATF deciding not to send any cases to the Eastern Judicial District Court. Neither the Court nor District Attorney wanted to try the case, but reluctantly agreed to do so. It turned out to be a real circus, and from the outset it did not look good for the good guys and got worse as things moved along. I recall commenting to Joe that if anybody went to jail it would probably be us.

After the state presented their evidence (and admittedly the case was weak), Percy himself took the stand and of course denied any involvement. He was allowed to speak to and attack (verbally) witnesses, officers and others sitting in the courtroom and to say pretty much anything he wanted to say. He pointed at me and said I saw that boy snooping around and trespassing on my property (it was not me but probably Dunn agent John Lorrick, who was about my age and size). The Preacher was of course the star witness and Percy's defense attorneys took him apart in their cross examination. They attacked his honesty and reliability, bringing out that he was paid a large reward for catching Percy (which was not true) and what was really more devastating that he had a long criminal record including felony convictions. Case over — all not guilty. I am sure the District Attorney did the best he could do with what he had and was certainly not aware of the Preacher's record. I don't think we (ATF) knew either, but we should have known and made the District Attorney aware of it.

Joshua Percy Flowers was, and remains today more than five decades after his moonshine empire, a legend in Johnston County and central and eastern North Carolina. To most of the Johnston County old-timers, he and actress Ava Gardner are the two most notable citizens of the county (Flowers was actually born in neighboring Wilson County). Both were buried in the Sunset Memorial Park in Smithfield, and both have everlasting monuments to their lives and deeds: the Percy Flowers Store and the wonderful Ava Gardner Museum in Smithfield. Upon his death in 1982 at the age of 79, it was reported Percy only had a few dollars in the bank but owned over 4,000 acres of prime land that he had acquired over the years beginning back in the Depression, primarily from making and selling moonshine liquor.

Today his daughter (his son was killed in an airplane crash in 1952 at the age of 24) owns the property and is developing it into commercial and residential properties. To most of the local people, Percy Flowers was a generous and caring man who took care of the less fortunate in the community — who like Robin Hood took from the rich (the government) and gave to the poor. And by all accounts he was a very generous man who did care for and give to the less fortunate. But, did he do it out of compassion for his fellow man or perhaps he had another motive? Maybe he foresaw a time when the poor man might be in a position to help him out or even might be on a jury. I do not know and maybe no one knows, but I suspect it might have been a little of both.

Reflecting on his long pursuit of Percy, Joe Carter came to the conclusion that Percy was a genius and would have been successful in any lawful business or enterprise he may have undertaken. He was smart and had a way with folks — through generosity and kindness or ruthlessness, if need be. In a number of cases we had enough evidence on him to convict the Pope, but the jury would turn him loose. He said that Percy, an avid dog breeder and hunter, once invited him to go hunting with him. Joe told Percy he would as long as he could walk behind him.

I was recently traveling near Smithfield and decided to stop at the Sunset Memorial Park Cemetery to view the gravesites of Percy Flowers and Ava Gardner. I located Ava's gravesite quickly, as there were signs directing visitors to its location. There were no directional signs to the Flowers gravesite, and after searching for twenty or thirty minutes I did not find it. As I walked back to my car, the thought crossed my mind that once again Percy had eluded the Federal man. I later discovered that Percy's remains had been removed to a private family cemetery located near The Percy Flowers Store.

Chapter Six
MOONSHINE AND MORE
(1971)

That Pesky Gun Stuff

As with most investigators, liquor enforcement was really what we wanted to pursue. However, the federal firearms laws were becoming more and more of something we *had* to do. The Gun Control Act of 1968 (GCA of 1968) was passed because of the assassinations of Robert Kennedy and Martin Luther King, both of which occurred in 1968. It was the first federal comprehensive gun law and, of course, was very controversial. Basically it did three things: 1) for the first time it gave federal oversight and regulation over the firearms industry by establishing a licensing system; 2) it prohibited certain individuals from buying and possessing firearms; and, 3) made certain firearms and destructive devices illegal to possess. ATF was given the enforcement and regulation responsibility of the law. At the outset there was very little effort on criminal enforcement, as gun violations were not considered very important by either the ATF or the federal courts. On the other hand, the regulatory requirements of the law did require significant time and effort.

The law required that all individuals and businesses dealing in firearms and ammunition had to be licensed and checked periodically for compliance. At that time there were only three or four compliance officers in the Charlotte District, and their focus was on regulating and collecting taxes on the tobacco and alcohol industry. Therefore, the regulatory responsibility for the licensing and compliance of the dealers was left to the criminal enforcement investigators. There were lots of dealers ranging from the small country stores to the large company chain stores, and each and every one had to have a background investigation prior to licensing and a yearly compliance investigation for renewal.

Investigator Devaney was assigned the task of managing the firearms licensing and compliance effort at Raleigh, which meant he would receive the assignments from the District office, assign them out to investigators in their respective counties, and return the completed reports to the District office. We, of course, gave these assignments the lowest priority and got to them when we could, and when we did get to it, our investigation was far less thorough and less time consuming than what ATF inspection officers do today. Some of the inspections now, I am told, can take days and sometime even weeks to complete, while ours probably averaged thirty minutes or less depending on the size of the dealer.

Generally, I think most licensees tried to understand and comply with the licensing and record keeping requirements, even though most didn't really see the need. There were a few who proved difficult even though you repeatedly explained the law, helped them set up their acquisition and disposition records, and showed them how to maintain the records. One example was a hardware store in Oxford that was owned and operated by an elderly gentleman. After several visits and attempts to help him, he finally told me he just didn't understand it and was not going to do it. I eventually, and reluctantly, recommended his license be revoked and it was. In another difficult case, there was a pawn shop in Durham where the records were never in order. Agent Devaney tried time and time again to get the owner to set up and maintain the required records without any success or apparent effort by the owner. Out of frustration, Devaney finally told him (and helped him) to take every gun off the shelves and to not make any more sales until his records were in order. A few weeks later the word came down from the District Office that Devaney should probably go back to the pawn shop and help put the guns back on the shelves. It seems the owner's brother had a friend who knew someone that knew the Regional Director (in another Region). As suggested, Don and I complied.

Relief from Disabilities
The GCA of 1968 provided that persons prohibited from possessing, shipping, transporting, or receiving firearms or ammunition could make application to the Secretary of the Treasury for relief from disabilities imposed by Federal laws with respect to the acquisition and possession of firearms. In other words, persons convicted of a felony could apply to have their rights restored to possess a firearm.

The application and required investigation were quite lengthy and detailed, covering not only the conviction, but many other aspects of the person's life and reputation as well. After completing all the interviews and gathering the pertinent information required, the assigned investigator prepared and submitted a report of investigation. The report contained not only their findings, but also their recommendation as to whether or not the relief should be granted. I never knew of a case where the investigator's recommendation was not followed, which in the vast majority of cases was to approve the restoration of rights.

While the Relief assignments were considered by some as yet another distraction, I think most realized its importance and made a conscientious effort to be thorough and fair. Probably the most noted Relief investigation involved former Vice President Spiro T. Agnew. He applied for, and was granted, relief after being convicted of tax evasion in the Watergate era. In the late '80s, Congress discontinued the allocation of funds for Relief investigations, which in effect eliminated the procedure of having firearms rights restored.

Explosives Law

In January, Devaney and I attended a week-long training session on the new explosives laws and ATF's regulation and enforcement. The law, Title XI of the Organized Crime Act was similar to the GCA of 1968 in that it required dealers in explosives to be licensed and maintain records as to the sale or disposition of explosives. The law also required individuals and companies dealing in or using explosives to have an approved storage facility to house their explosives. Just as with the gun laws, criminal enforcement again had the licensing and inspection responsibility. There were far fewer explosives dealers and users, so the task was not as time consuming, and I think we gave it a little more importance and emphasis than in the case of the firearms effort. But again, it was just another distraction from our primary job of working illicit liquor.

Still in the Living Room

In February, working with State ABC Officer John Britt, Vance County ABC officers T. Blackmon and Bill Watkins, and Granville

County ABC officer Arthur Ray Currin, we located and seized a large distillery in Vance County. The still was actually set up in the living room and two bedrooms of a modern type ranch house in a middle-income neighborhood in Henderson, and parts of the distillery could be seen from the street. The occupants of the home, Vincent Travis and his wife, were arrested. The 960-gallon metal vat still with 900 gallons of mash was seized and destroyed along with 40 gallons of nontax paid whiskey. Some two months later, Travis was arrested again in Granville County while running a 480-gallon submarine still.

Curtis Lee O'Neal

In March, I assisted Wake County ABC officer Buzzy Anthony in the execution of a state search warrant at the residence of Curtis Lee O'Neal on Kearney Road in Wake Forest. We found and seized various distillery materials (not set up) and one gallon of nontax paid whiskey. I recall O'Neal as being a young, clean-cut man with a wife and young child—certainly not the image of a notorious moonshiner. Well, first impressions can certainly be misleading, and in this instance were very much so. Over the next few months, O'Neal went big time in the moonshine business and later graduated to breaking and entering and burglary. He was convicted of breaking and entering and safecracking in 1975, felony larceny in 1977, assault with a deadly weapon with intent to kill in 1988, and trafficking in marijuana in 1993. He eventually wound up in Wilkes County, and was found in possession of firearms in 1994. Special Agent Driver of the Greensboro ATF Office conducted an investigation relative to the incident and charged him with violations of the federal firearms. He was convicted in 1995 and sentenced to 262 months in federal prison under the Armed Career Criminal provisions.

Bud Lowery

In March, we seized a large distillery in the Wilder's Store section of Franklin County. The seizure consisted of four 1,350-gallon metal tanks stills, 2,400 gallons of mash, and 314 gallons of nontax paid whiskey. Spencer Duke "Bud" Lowery and Willie Douglas Barnes were arrested while operating the still. Lowery either had bad luck or was not very good at looking out for the law, as he was caught a number of times during the early seventies. He lived in a small house across from Mays Store at the Franklin- Granville county line. A number of times, I conducted surveillance of his house in the very early mornings to see if he was leaving. When a pattern of him leaving was established, ATF pilot Marshall Reece was called in for aerial surveillance. We located two or three stills by following Lowery, one of which was a large distillery just off I-85 near the Virginia line. To this day, I don't think he and several other moonshiners were ever aware of how the airplane was used to locate distilleries.

Lowery was a likable fellow with a sense of humor. One day when I was walking along the highway back to my car after I had walked out a large wooded area near Youngsville, Lowery drove by. He stopped and we talked a few minutes, and I asked him to give me a ride back to my car (I needed a ride and thought maybe I might be able to get some information from him). He said he would like to but couldn't, because if he was seen with me it would not look good and might "harm his reputation".

A state probation officer told me about an interesting experience he had with Lowery. He said that Lowery was in state prison on liquor charges and had just a few months remaining on his sentence. As part of his job, he talked with Lowery and told him if he would promise not to go back to making moonshine he thought he could get him out of prison early. Lowery, after a little thought, said, "I really can't promise you that because within a few days of me getting out I'll be back on some creek bank making liquor". You really have to admire his honesty.

Coy Pleasants Jr.

Coy Jr., as he was known, was a close associate of Lowery and very active in the moonshine business, as his family had been for years. They ran and operated their moonshine business out of their country store near Youngsville. We found and destroyed several liquor stashes in and around the store and arrested Coy Jr. a number of times making and transporting moonshine. His brother Fleming Macon Pleasants (Buddy Boy) was probably the brains of their operation and a little more difficult to catch. We only caught him one time. He was later convicted of drug trafficking and sentenced to life in prison. He died in 2005 at the age of 66. Coy Jr. died three years earlier in 2002.

Kenneth Horton

Another interesting Franklin County bootlegger was Kenneth Horton. Like Lowery and Pleasants, he was a still hand and transporter, and a fellow with a little bad luck but also a good sense of humor, even in some bad times. In June, I received information from an informer that Horton was going the next day to Wilkes County to pick up a load of liquor and would be returning in the afternoon. According to the informer, he would be driving a white Oldsmobile (a known liquor car that we had seen at his house).

Investigator Devaney and I met with Orange County ABC officers Burch Compton and Paul Cook and set up surveillance on I-85 in Orange County. At approximately 2:00 p.m. we observed the Oldsmobile pass traveling east on I-85. We followed the vehicle and pulled up alongside, at which time I observed Horton driving the vehicle and numerous plastic jugs could be seen in the rear seat area of the car. I motioned for him to pull over and he started to slow down and pull over, but as we pulled in behind him, he took off at a high rate of speed. We pursued him along I-85, and after a short chase, he abruptly turned off the highway, crossed an open field area and disappeared over an embankment. I thought for sure he had driven off into a lake or river down below.

Whatever his fate, we too were about to experience it, as Burch followed right in his tracks and over the embankment we went. Fortunately for him and us, it was not a lake but a dirt service road that ran along the Interstate about 10 to 12 feet below the elevation of the highway. After we came to a stop, Don and I exited the vehicle and arrested Horton after a short foot chase. We found and seized 232 gallons of liquor in gallon plastic jugs located in the rear seat and trunk area of the car.

Less than a month later, I found 150 gallons of moonshine stashed in a wooded area a short distance from Horton's home. The next day, Horton drove into the area and started loading the jugs into the trunk of his car. As Devaney and I walked up to either side of the car to arrest Horton, I believe I said to him something to the effect, "It's good to see you again." He laughed and said, "I was looking forward to seeing you again, but not quite so soon".

The next day as we were processing him at the ATF office, he was telling stories and laughing as if he was not a prisoner but just one of the guys. I recall Area Supervisor Lawson walked into the room wearing his tailored suit and Horton saying to him, "Hey, I know you. Did we go to college together or did I meet you in prison?" I heard later that Kenneth had committed suicide.

Al Henderson

Henderson was a black moonshiner who lived and made liquor in Vance and Warren counties. His stills were usually close to Kerr Lake and sometimes could only be accessed by boat from the lake. He was pretty slick and one of the few moonshiners I ever encountered who actually used countermeasures to detect the presence of officers. He would sometimes surround the still area with small twine and check to see if had been broken before going to the still.

On one occasion we were working his still when he walked up on us with a horse bridle in his hands. When questioned by Mike, he maintained he didn't know anything about the nearby still; he was just looking for his old mule that had gotten out of the barn. Al usually did not run the still, but had his sons and other relatives working for him. We caught one of sons, Leon, and a cousin at one still but another time the boys outran us. They were young and very fast and all we caught was a pair of tennis shoes that they had discarded or just ran out of them.

Back to Wilkesboro

In June, Mike told me that I was going to Wilkes County for some cross training. It was not unusual for agents from the western part of the state to come east and vice versa of for training. Upon arrival, I was told that the Wilkes County agents were sitting on a large stash of moonshine in a barn at the residence of Ardle Darnell, and old-time bootlegger in Ashe County. The plan was for me and the others brought in to relieve the agents currently on the ground watching the barn.

As was the practice in the area, it would be necessary to drop us off a long-distance from the site and walk to the location. I really did not relish the idea of walking up and down the mountains. Just as we were getting ready to drop off, the agents on the ground radioed that they were going to raid the barn. I was told to go to a crossroads a short distance away and pick up an officer who was there making observations at that intersection. Upon arrival, I saw the scruffy looking fellow coming out of the woods and I recalled thinking, "Who is this redneck?" It was Phil McGuire, a Regional Investigator out of Atlanta, the ace undercover agent that I heard so much about in ATF basic school.

We traveled to the residence, at which time I learned that the agents had raided the barn and seized about 3,000 gallons of non-tax paid whiskey. I learned that Darnell was an old-time moonshiner who had been caught and served time previously. He was the old timey moonshiner who took great pride in his whiskey. He actually built his stills himself including making his barrels. I observed some of the barrel staves and metal rings that he used to make the barrels.

I met the Wilkesboro agents and others who were there to assist in the investigation. One of the agents, Sam Cabe, an old timer with a colorful history and reputation said that he could probably find the distillery from which the liquor came. I recall riding with him up and down and around the mountains until we came to a point where a dirt logging road came out of the woods onto the highway. Sam said, "Boys, your still is in there." We drove in and, sure enough, found a very large distillery.

During this time and subsequently, I learned that agent McGuire had located the stash by following a load of raw materials (sugar/jugs) from another state to the area. Either in undercover capacity or the utilization of confidential source, McGuire was responsible for locating a number of large distilleries in Tennessee and North Carolina.

Super B

In 1968, Chrysler Motors came out with the Dodge Super Bee, a relatively low- priced muscle car. It looked fast, and it was fast with a powerful Hemi engine. An orange one with a load of liquor was seized and put into service by the Dunn agents, and later transferred to the Raleigh office and assigned to Special Agent Stanfill.

And so it was one early morning in August, we were working a previously located liquor stash in the Flat Rock Church section of Franklin County. Agent Burroughs and I were on the ground observing the liquor and Stanfill (in the Super Bee) and Devaney were in cars. The plan was that once the liquor was loaded in the violator's car, Stanfill would pick us up, and we would follow and arrest the violator and seize the liquor and his vehicle.

And sure enough as expected, at about 4:30 am Louis Vaughan came to the stash, loaded some of the jugs in his car and departed. As planned, Stanfill picked us up and we started after Vaughan at a high rate of speed to try to catch up. As we were approaching Franklinton and had yet to seen Vaughan's car, Stanfill goosed it a bit and lost it. The Super Bee was out of control and each time it switched ends I could see Hart's Store, and we were headed straight toward it. We were surely going to slam into the store, or worse, slide through the intersection of Highway 56 and be hit broadsided. Stanfill stayed with it and we eventually came to a stop in a shallow ditch.

I'm not sure if it was Stanfill's driving ability or just fate, but was glad we were not hurt and there was no damage to the car. After regaining our composure, we continued on to where Agent Devaney had stopped and arrested Vaughan with 60 gallons of liquor in his car.

Charles Langley

Charles Langley was a Major Violator who lived in Nash County and, like a lot of the moonshiners, came from moonshining families. His father Sid Langley had been a Major Violator and had made liquor for years.

In November 1970, Kentucky State Police stopped a truck loaded with 1,400 gallons of moonshine whiskey. The driver of the truck, Raymond Medlin of Rocky Mount, was a known associate of Langley. Subsequent investigation and surveillance led Rocky Mount and Goldsboro agents to a large farm in Marengo, Indiana, where they found and seized a large distillery. The distillery with a mash capacity of 12,000 gallon (sixty-seven 180-gallon barrels) used metal tank stills and steam boilers, and produced 1,200-1,400 gallons of liquor per run. Sid Langley and another man were pres-

Mike Zetts, Investigator in Charge, Raleigh ATF Office.

Assisant Regional Commissioner Bill Griffin presenting the Southeast Regional Pistol Match trophy to the Charlotte Pistol Team, 1971. Pictured l-r: Bob Powell, Charlie Favre, Leonard Mika, Bill Griffin, Roger Brown, and Ronnie Williams. Courtesy of Charlie Favre.

Treasury Law Enforcement School No. 639
Enforcement Law and Criminal Investigation
September 23 - November 1969
The Department of the Treasury
Washington, D.C.

A. T. & F. Basic Investigators School No. 28
National Training Center
January 6 - January 30, 1970

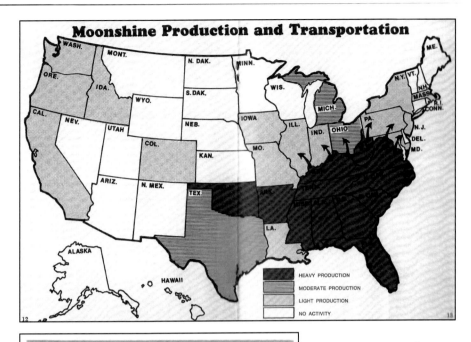

Moonshine Production and Transportation

HEAVY PRODUCTION
MODERATE PRODUCTION
LIGHT PRODUCTION
NO ACTIVITY

STILL SEIZURES 1969

STATE	TOTAL STATE AND LOCAL	FEDERAL	TOTAL FEDERAL, STATE AND LOCAL
ALABAMA	1,833	804	2,637
ARKANSAS	7	41	48
CALIFORNIA	0	4	4
COLORADO	2	0	2
FLORIDA	90	88	178
GEORGIA	1,745	1,187	2,932
IDAHO	0	1	1
ILLINOIS	0	4	4
INDIANA	0	5	5
IOWA	1	0	1
KENTUCKY	9	89	98
LOUISIANA	1	10	11
MARYLAND	6	2	8
MASSACHUSETTS	0	1	1
MICHIGAN	1	33	34
MISSISSIPPI	354	207	561
MISSOURI	0	1	1
NEW JERSEY	4	0	4
NEW YORK	0	2	2
NORTH CAROLINA	619	786	1,405
OHIO	8	11	19
OKLAHOMA	1	49	50
OREGON	1	1	2
PENNSYLVANIA	9	0	9
SOUTH CAROLINA	333	340	673
TENNESSEE	196	359	555
TEXAS	7	17	24
VIRGINIA	260	64	324
WASHINGTON	3	2	5
WEST VIRGINIA	18	31	49
TOTAL	5,508	4,139	9,647

Above: Moonshine Production and Distribution Chart, 1969. Courtesy of Licensed Beverage Industries (LBI, Inc.).

Left: List of distillery seizures by state, 1969. Courtesy of LBI, Inc.

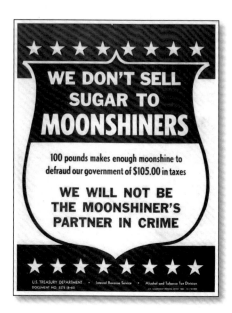

Through the years ATF has used posters and other novelties to warn the public of the dangers of moonshine.

June 16, 1970

TOP TWENTY LIST - MAJOR VIOLATORS

NORTH CAROLINA

POSITION ON LIST	NAME OF MAJOR VIOLATOR	ASSIGNED TO	ESTIMATED WKLY VOLUME	JUDICIAL DISTRICT
Raleigh 1.	DORSEY, Louis	Thomas W. Stokes	3,600	Eastern
2.	BURGESS, Ralph "Puff"	Owen D. Bean	3,000	Western & Middle
Dunn 3.	JOHNSON, Allen Ray	James H. Lumpkin	2,500	Eastern
Raleigh 4.	ROSS, Douglas Freeman	Thomas W. Stokes	2,400	Eastern
Wilkes 5.	VICKERS, Hubert E.	Edwin O. Hazelip	2,400	Middle
Raleigh 6.	COOLEY, C. V.	William S. Walien	2,200	Eastern
Dunn 7.	FLOWERS, Joshua Percy	Ronald E. Williams	2,000	Eastern
Wilkes 8.	THARPE, Willie James	Thomas L. Chapman	1,700	Middle
9.	JOHNSON, Calvin Spurgeon	Robert G. Martin	1,500	Western & Middle
Wilkes 10.	COLBERT, Fred	George R. Powell	1,400	Middle
Ry. mt 11.	LANGLEY, Sidney Ross	Carl D. Bowers	1,200	Eastern
Win Sale 12.	ASHLEY, Millard Franklin	John W. Harrell	1,200	Middle
13.	STALEY, Ransom Tenson	Bruce R. Bassett	1,200	Middle
Win Sale 14.	GRAY, John Ross	Aubrey M. Huffman	1,000	Middle
Wilkes 15.	BILLINGS, Don	Thomas L. Chapman	1,000	Middle
Raleigh 16.	POOLE, Donald Reed	Donald R. Devaney	900	Middle
17.	LEE, Furman Cortez	Samuel P. Turnbull, Jr.	800	Middle
18.	WILLIAMS, Dwight "Bud"	Bruce R. Bassett	700	Middle
Goldsb 19.	WHALEY, George "Bossy"	Ralph A. Ellis	660	Eastern
Raleigh 20.	FIELDS, Lonless E.	Joseph Kopka	650	Eastern

North Carolina Major Violator List, June 16, 1970.

SOUTHEAST REGION ILLICIT DISTILLERY SURVEY ESTIMATES

Thru Channels to: Chief, Enf. Br., ATF	DATE: January 14, 1971

The following estimate of distilleries is reported based upon the best information, knowledge and belief that can be determined jointly by the personnel assigned to this post of duty.

STATE	COUNTY	POST OF DUTY	JUDICIAL DISTRICT
North Carolina	Franklin	Raleigh	Eastern - N.C.

NO.	NAMES OF OWNERS	SOURCE (INF OR MO)	TOTAL MASH CAPACITY (Gals.)	LOCATION
1	Douglas Freeman Ross	MO	15,000	State wide and Virginia
2	Louis Bean Dorsey	INF	15,000	State wide
3	Lelon North Winstead (Chick)	INF	7,000	Franklin & Nash Co.
4	Fleming Macon Pleasants (Buddyboy)	MO	5,000	County wide
5	Lafayette Johnson	INF	2,500	County wide
6	James Wrenn	MO	1,000	Moulton Sec.
7	Ronald Mitchell	MO	900	Pocomoke Sec.
8	Lacy Louis Inscoe	INF	500	White Level Sec.
9	Roscoe Joyner	MO	500	Bunn Sec.
10	Parker Robbins	MO	500	Louisburg T.P.
11	James Lancaster	INF	500	Centerville Sec.
12	E. P. Privette	MO	500	Bunn & Pilot Sec.
13	Verris Cooper	MO	300	Bunn & Pilot Sec.

49,250

Franklin Co.
- 49,250

13

Total mash 97,550
Number of Violators 48

SIGNATURE (Investigator in Charge)	INITIALS (Area Supervisor)

DEPARTMENT OF THE TREASURY
INTERNAL REVENUE SERVICE

RC SE FORM ATF - 243 (REV. 7-69)

Southeast Region Illicit Distillery Survey Estimates (ATLIDS), Franklin County, NC, January 14, 1971.

Copper pot type still seized in Nash County, NC. Courtesy of Ed Garrison.

Two submarine type stills seized in the Hurricanes section of Wake County, NC. Courtesy of Charlie Favre.

Buzzy Anthony with two submarine stills seized near Wake Forest. Courtesy of Buzzy Anthony.

These two submarine stills were observed for a few days. No one ever came, so the stills were cut up with an axe! Courtesy of Buzzy Anthony.

Four metal tank stills seized in Franklin County, NC, April 1971. Pictured l-r: ATF Agent Johnny Binkley and ABC Officer Buzzy Anthony.

Percy Flowers 100-barrel steam still seized in Johnston County, NC, November 1967. Courtesy of Buzzy Anthony.

Four metal tank stills seized during an operation in Franklin County, April 21, 1971. Pictured l-r: the defendant, Wake ABC Officer Buzzy Anthony, Franklin County Chief Deputy David Batton, and ATF Agents Mike Zetts and Johnny Binkley.

Bud Lowery
Willie D. Barnes

INVENTORY
ILLEGAL DISTILLERY **21** APRIL 1971

4	1350 gallon steel vats (stills)
2400	gallons of fermenting mash
314	gallons of NTPL
18	100# butane gas tanks
1	500 gallon cooler box w/2 radiator condensors
2	55 gallon metal caps
3	55 gallon wooden doubler kegs
1	115 gallon liquor barrel
2	#3 wash tubs
100	lbs of bran flakes
7	55 gallon metal liquor barrels
2	55 gallon metal barrels (trash)
2	galvinized burners
40	ft. gas line connector hose
4	cases (240) 1gallon plastic jugs
10	cases (60) 1 gallon plastic jugs (trunk of Chev Auto)
400	ft. 1½ " plastic hose
100	ft. 2" plastic hose
1	pick
1	hoe
1	shovel
1	pitchfork
1	Briggs/Stratton 3 hp. motor w/wtr pump attached
2	hand filters
1	10 qt bucket
1	12 by 24 tarp
1	15 by 25 tarp
1	1962 Chev Auto 1971 Lic # CY 8156

ATF Agent L.C. Puryear prepairing explosive charges to destroy a large still seized in Franklin County, NC. Courtesy of Charlie Favre.

Large submarine still seized in Franklin County, NC. Pictured l-r: ATF Agent Oscar Vaughan, Wake County ABC Officer Jim Burnette, ATF Agents Bob Furr and Charlie Favre, and Wake County ABC Officer Tommy Jeffries. Courtesy of Charlie Favre.

Raleigh ATF Supervisor Oscar Vaughan in training class in October 1958. Vaughan later died of a heart attack while changing a tire on his ATF car. Courtesy of Charlie Favre.

ATF Agent Larry Burkhalter examining a large sill seized in Franklin County, NC. Courtesy of Charlie Favre.

Wake County ABC Chief Jim Burnette catches a large one. Courtesy of Charlie Favre.

Granville County ABC Chief Arthur Ray Currin (left) and ATF Agent Bobby Sherrill (right) at a still in Granville County. Courtesy of Buzzy Anthony.

Moonhiner at work. Courtesy of Charlie Favre.

Two officers destroying sugar seized at a large still in Wake County, NC. Courtesy of Charlie Favre.

Mash boxes rigged with detonating cord and explosive charges to destroy a large still in Magnolia, NC. Courtesy of Ed Garrison.

Unidentified deputy at two submarine stills in Granville County, NC.

Right: ATF Agent Johnny Binkley doing the paperwork following the seizure of a large still in Franklin County.

Below: Large still seized in the Wood section of Franklin County, 1969. Courtesy of The Franklin Times.

Scenes Of Monday Night's Still Raid Staff photos by Astor Bowden.

Revenuer Loses Cuffs, Prisoner But Finds Both

A Monday night raid on a small whisky still in the Pilot section of Franklin County 10 miles south of here by federal agent Mike Zetts resulted in the temporary loss of a pair of handcuffs and two prisoners.

Zetts walked up on the 200-gallon submarine type still unnoticed by the two men working there until he announced that they were under arrest. He handcuffed the older man to a tree and while doing so the younger man took flight.

Zetts gave chase but was no match for the youth. When Zetts returned to the tree where the older man had been handcuffed, he was surprised to find out that he too had disappeared,

having climbed up the small tree and made good his escape in that manner.

On Tuesday, Franklin County Sheriff W. T. Dement had a visitor. Verus Cooper of Rt. 2, Zebulon, returned the handcuffs and identified the two missing booze makers as his son, Verus Cooper Jr., 18, and his brother, Sandy Bell Cooper, 48, both of Rt. 2, Zebulon.

Federal agents arrived at the courthouse a short time later and Zetts recovered his handcuffs. Warrants were issued against the two men who were placed in the county jail in lieu of $500 bond each on whisky making charges.

The Durham Morning Herald

Newspaper article regarding the escape of a prisoner with ATF Agent Mike Zetts' handcuffs at a still raid in Franklin County, NC. Courtesy of the Durham Morning Herald.

Picture of a large still in Franklin County before and after destruction by explosives. Courtesy of The Franklin Times, Louisburg, NC.

1,001 gallons of moonshine seized in a tobacco barn in Granville County, NC, May 1970. Pictured l-r: ATF Agents Stan Burroughs and Johnny Binkley.

Officers destroying 1,001 gallons of moonshine in Granville County, NC. Pictured l-r: ATF Agent Johnny Binkley and Granville ABC Chief Arthur Currin.

SHERIFF DEMENT, DEPUTY SHERIFF GUPTON AT STILL SITE

Big Operation

Officers Capture "Granddaddy" Still

Sheriff William T. Dement has reported the capture of what he termed a "granddaddy" whiskey still in the Alert section of Franklin County. Dement said it was an unusually large operation.

Sheriff's officers and federal ATU officers dynamited the huge layout Tuesday afternoon. No arrests were made, but officers are continuing their investigations.

Dement reported that two 940-gallon stills were destroyed along with eight 1,125-gallon stills. In addition, 7,800 gallons of mash was destroyed. Confiscated at the site were 2 gallons of whiskey, 3,000 pounds of sugar, 1,350 one-gallon plastic jugs, and two

vehicles.

Officers took a 1956 Ford pickup truck and a 1948 Chevrolet one-ton truck.

In addition, there were a number of propane gas tanks and other assorted materials used in the illegal operation. Dement's department unloaded three trucks of materials here Wednesday

morning.

One report theorized that some fittings which escaped destruction were lifted by the still operators after officers left the scene Tuesday. When officers returned later, the copper fittings were missing. The operation was discovered in a heavily wooded area between Alert and Epsom.

Arrest photograph of major violator Douglas F. Ross in Franklin County on liquor law violations, 1971.

Submarine stills seized in Wake County on Hwy 50 N. Pictured l-r: Wake County ABC Officers Merritt and Anthony, and ATF Agents Favre and Vaughan. Courtesy of Buzzy Anthony.

317 gallons of moonshine seized at the residence of Parker Robbins in Franklin County, April 1971. Courtesy of Buzzy Anthony.

Large still found in the woods in Franklin County, NC.

Large still seized in the Riley Hill section of Wake County, NC, 1969. Courtesy of Buzzy Anthony.

Charlotte Pistol Team, 1971. Pictured l-r: Roger Brown, Charlie Favre, Ronnie Williams, and Bob Powell. Courtesy of Charlie Favre.

UPTON   BRAWLEY   DEMENT   BATTON   TERRELL   STOKES

Officers Get A Really Big One

Sheriff William T. Dement's department and ATU officers captured a really big one last Thursday night near Pilot in Franklin County. Dement reports that a steam-type 600-gallon capacity still was raided last Thursday night around 9 p.m. He gave the location as 3 miles southwest of Pilot near Rocky Cross and the Nash County line.

Two men were arrested at the site, Dement said. They were identified as Jimmy Allen Fuller, w/m/26 of Route 1, Louisburg and Walter Perry, w/m/26 of Route 2, Wake Forest. Both will be tried in Franklin District Court on December 8, according to the Sheriff.

Dement reported that his deputies and ATU officers returned to the site Friday morning and destroyed it. Found at the still was a 7-foot upright boiler, forty 180-gallon barrels of mash and fifteen 60-gallon barrels and a total of 4450 gallons of mash. There were 330 gallons of finished whiskey discovered at the site, Dement said. Confiscated in the raid was a 1964, ¾ ton Ford truck, 3 water pumps, 46 cases of jars and 2,000 pounds of coal.   *Photo Courtesy of T. H. Pearce.*

Newspaper article relating to a large steam still seized in the Pilot section of Franklin County, 1969. Courtesy of the Franklin Times, Louisburg, NC.

"Largest Still In Years" Captured Monday

Franklin Sheriff William T. Dement reports the capture of what ATU officer Mike Zetts described as "the largest distillery seized in Franklin County in several years" late Monday afternoon near Bunn. Dement's department and ATU officers raided the operation around 4:30 P.M. The 548-gallon daily output booze business was destroyed by the officers.

Two arrests were made as officers outdistanced the operators in a 100-yard dash. Jimmy Ray Jeffreys, 29, and Donald Eugene Jeffreys, 28, both of Route 4, Louisburg were captured at the site and charged with operating a distillery and possession of materials for the manufacture of whiskey.

Zetts reported that the two men are brothers and that they were caught in a heavily wooded area about 100-yards from the still after a foot race.

Dement said the raid netted 276 gallons of nontax paid liquor, 2250 gallons of mash, 195 55-gallon barrels, one 600-gallon tank still, one 1550-gallon submarine type still, four 600-gallon sub type stills and one 7 ft. low-pressure boiler.

The raid occurred just off State rural road 1608 near Hall's Crossroads on NC-39. The distillery was described by officers as having a 13,450-gallon capacity.

Still Raided, Wrecked

Federal and Sheriff's officers are shown above destroying a huge illegal whiskey distillery Monday afternoon near Bunn. Man at far left is unidentified. Others left to right are: Don Devaney and Mike Zetts, special agents of the Alcohol and Firearms Division of the U. S. Treasury Department, Deputy John Deal and Sheriff William T. Dement. The 13,450-gallon capacity operation was described as the largest captured in the county in several years. Staff photo by Astor Bowden.

Newspaper article and photo of a large still seized near Bunn in Franklin County, NC. Pictured l-r: ATF Agents Devaney and Zetts, Franklin County Deputy Deal, and Sheriff Dement. Courtesy of the Franklin Times.

Published Every Tuesday & Thursday

Telephone 496-3283   Ten Cents   Louisburg, N. C., Thursday, March 11,

Truckload Of Booze

Law officers are shown above inspecting truck load of non-tax paid whiskey captured near Mitchiner's Crossroads Tuesday. Pictured, left to right, are ATFD agent Buzzy Anthony, Franklin Sheriff William T. Dement and ATFD agent Tommy Stokes. Dement reports 78 gallons of illegal booze was taken and the truck confiscated. He reports that Coy M. Pleasants Jr., 29, Rt. 3, Wake Forest was arrested and charged with transportation of non-tax paid whiskey. Trial is set for April 5.

Seizure of a truck loaded with seventy-eight gallons of moonshine in March 1971 in Franklin County; Coy Pleasants Jr. was arrested. Pictured l-r: ABC Officer Buzzy Anthony, Sheriff Dement, and ATF Agent Tommy Stokes. Courtesy of The Franklin Times.

Home of Herman Harris with outbuilding in the rear located on US-1 in Franklinton, NC. Courtesy of Billy Dement.

Franklinton Booze Factory

Scene above shows Sheriff's officers and ATTU officers at illegal whiskey still captured at Franklinton Wednesday. Pictured, t to right, are: Franklin Sheriff William T. Dement, Chief Deputy Sheriff David Batton, ATU officer John Spidel, Deputy in Deal, and ATU officer Bobby Sherrill. Dement reports the arrest of Herman Harris, c/m/37, owner of the home where the l was found. Harris is charged with manufacture, possession and transportation of non-tax-paid whiskey. Three imarine-type stills were discovered in a shed behind the house which sits near US 1 at Franklinton. Dement said two were in eration and that officers confiscated 1300 gallon of mash, 48 gallons of illegal booze, a quantity of rubbing alcohol, which s used to spike the moonshine and Harris' 1969 Ford XL which was loaded with several cases of whiskey. A hearing was set December 7 in the case.

-Photo by T. H. Pearce.

Submarine still found in the Harris outbuilding in Franklinton. Courtesy of Billy Dement.

Large sub-stills seized in the Seven Paths section of Franklin County. Courtesy of Billy Dement.

Large sub-still showing the condenser and catch barrel in stream. Courtesy of Billy Dement.

Wilkesboro ATF investigators in the 1960s. Pictured l-r: Kolen Flack, Haywood Weddle, Bill Queen Sr., Robert Schmidt, Joe Carter, P.H. "Bull" Blettner. Courtesy of Phil Carter.

Cover of the Saturday Evening Post, August 2, 1958 edition, story of Percy Flowers - King of the Moonshiners.

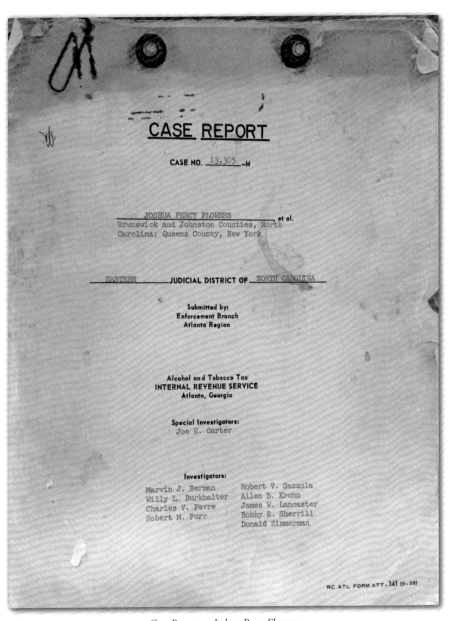

CASE REPORT

CASE NO. 13,305 -M

JOSHUA PERCY FLOWERS , et al.
Brunswick and Johnston Counties, North
Carolina; Queens County, New York

EASTERN JUDICIAL DISTRICT OF NORTH CAROLINA

Submitted by:
Enforcement Branch
Atlanta Region

Alcohol and Tobacco Tax
INTERNAL REVENUE SERVICE
Atlanta, Georgia

Special Investigators:
Joe E. Carter

Investigators:

Marvin J. Berman   Robert V. Gazzola
Willy L. Burkhalter   Allen B. Krohn
Charles V. Favre   James W. Lancaster
Robert M. Furr   Bobby E. Sherrill
                       Donald Zimmerman

RC ATL FORM ATT - 141 (9-58)

Case Report on Joshua Percy Flowers.

Still operated by Percy Flowers seized in Brunswick County, NC, 1963, with 80 mash vats containing 16,000 gallons of fermenting mash. Courtesy of Phil Carter.

Mash boxes at the Percy Flowers site. Courtesy of Phil Carter.

Cases of jars. Courtesy of Phil Carter.

Two radiator condensers at the Percy Flowers site. Courtesy of Phil Carter.

Photo of the Percy Flowers Store, located on NC 42 in Johnston County, NC, 2020.

Footstone at Ava Gardner's gravesite, Smithfield, NC.

Above and below: Wilkes County steam distillery with two boilers. Courtesy of Phil Carter.

1ces

1ns

and for no other purpose. That all parking areas shall be confined to that portion of the property lying north of the

...by the town would first assure the restoration of a historic home and second provide a suitable site for the location of a badly needed municipal

Hillsborough for its size and the remains of once beautiful gardens.
The home is now badly deteriorated and has been vacant for many years.

A Believe-It-Or-Not

B. Earle Bradsher reports an unusual event that took place at the home of his brother recently

advantage of the lines is that they ted to produce les and demands

iland, both sons ly attended a in Charlotte he double knit

goes into name of the Knitting Co. hosiery plant y Mill Inc. resident of

ig facility They are d sold to a After this kaged and name.

He says that one night his brother J. E. Bradsher, who lives just off Highway 86 north of Hillsborough, heard a strange noise just after going to bed. He arose and began looking for the source of the noise that seemed to be coming from the area of an oil circulator. After searching for a while Bradsher opened the door of the stove and found inside a live wild mallard (or duck). He removed the bird from the circulator and found it unharmed. After keeping the bird for several days he released it.

Apparently the bird entered the chimney at the Bradsher home during a storm that occurred about that time and soon thereafter found himself in the oil circulator.

ABC CHIEF BURCH COMPTON, left, and Orange Deputy Howard Watkins examine some of the non-tax paid whiskey captured last Wednesday just off Interstate 85 between Efland and Hillsborough.

Car Loaded With 232 Gallons
Of White Lightning Captured

A Franklin County farmer was captured Wednesday of last week about a half mile east of the Efland exit on I-85 in a car loaded with 232 gallons of white lightning.

Orange County ABC Police Chief Burch Compton and members of his force joined federal Alcohol, Tobacco and Firearms agents Johnny Binkley and Don DeVaney in a chase along Interstate 85, across a field and through a pine thicket to capture the load of non-taxpaid whiskey.

Compton said that he and the officers got behind the 1967 automobile driven by Kenneth Horton, 32, traveling towards Hillsborough on I-85 west of Efland. The driver ignored the officers' signals to pull over and a chase ensued.

"Then, Horton pulled off like he was going to stop, but drove down a flat area beside the highway and kept going. We followed in our car. He kept going through an area of pine trees and we kept following. He came to a stop when his car went down an embankment.

"When the car stopped, he jumped out and ran on foot, but was caught by Officer Binkley and DeVaney," Compton reported.

Horton was taken to Durham, where he appeared briefly before U. S. Commissioner Richard Hutson.
He was released on $400 bond for his

appearance at a hearing the September term of U. S. Middle District Court in Durham.

The officers, who confiscated the illicit whiskey, all of which was in plastic gallon jugs, for evidence and took the remainder of the cache to the Hillsborough landfill where it was destroyed.

Chief Compton said there was "very little" damage to the cars as a result of the chase through the wooded area.

Newspaper article on the arrest and seizure of 232 gallons of moonshine in Orange County, NC, June 1971.

ent and arrested when the still was raided. Charles and his father were subsequently convicted in Federal Court in Indiana.

The body of Raymond Medlin (the truck driver) was later found in an abandoned well near Rocky Mount, having been shot twice with a shotgun. No one was ever arrested for the murder, but Charles Langley was considered the primary suspect after it was learned that Medlin had threatened to testify against Langley unless he was paid $5,000 to keep quiet (two shotgun shells cost a lot less than $5,000).

While awaiting his appeal and sentencing in the Indiana case, Langley continued to go full steam ahead in the moonshine business. In October 1973, ATF agents and local officers found and seized a large distillery in the Magnolia section of Duplin County. The distillery consisted of two 500-gallon steel tanks fired by a steam boiler, numerous mash boxes and barrels, and 430 gallons of moonshine whiskey. With a mash capacity of 17,000 gallons, it was one of the largest stills ever seized in eastern North Carolina.

The still was located on a farm owned by a local high school principal. The principal, three still hands and Langley were arrested and tried in federal court. The day after the seizure, a truck loaded with 42 gallons of moonshine from the still was seized in Brooklyn, New York. As with Doug Ross and many other moonshiners, Langley turned to selling drugs after completing his federal sentence. And he, too, would cross paths with ATF agents again and as with Ross, things would not end well for him.

Claude Vance Cooley

Claude Vance (CV) Cooley was a Major Violator who lived and operated out of his mobile home park in Wake County. He had been a major violator of the liquor laws, with several arrests and convictions dating back to the 1950s.

I recall in Treasury School one of the instructors (a former ATF agent in New York) asking the class if there was anyone in here from "RILEY, NC?" and I of course raised my hand. He then asked if I knew Claude Vance Cooley and I, like most young agents wanting to appear knowledgeable and a little important, said I did (I had heard his name and knew that he was a major violator). He went on to tell how he had caught Cooley in New York City in the late

1950s with a load of moonshine. Being a little skeptical by nature, I pulled Cooley's rap sheet when I got back to "RILEY" and, sure enough, it showed an arrest for possession and transportation of non-tax-paid whiskey on 1-11-60 in Brooklyn, NY.

In the mid to late 1960s, he and Doug Ross, separately and sometimes together, put up a number of large stills in Wake, Franklin and Granville counties. Wake County ABC Officer W.H. "Buzzy" Anthony and Granville County ABC Officer Arthur Ray Currin—working with Raleigh ATF agents—found, seized and destroyed a number of Cooley's big stills. Buzzy tells the story about one of CV's big stills they worked in Wake County.

After watching the still a few days with no activity, they discontinued the surveillance with the idea to go back periodically and check it. Shortly after pulling off the still, Buzzy said he got a call from an informant telling him that they (moonshiners) were going back to the still. As a result, he and the other officers quickly returned to the still and shortly after getting there, a young, black youth came to the still. When they grabbed him, he told them that CV had given him $5 to go to the still to see if anyone was there. Mike Zetts said, "Okay, I will give you $10 to go back and tell them you didn't see anyone at the still."

He did, and a short time later, the moonshiners came to the still and were all arrested.

In another Cooley-Ross still investigation, ABC Office Currin tells the story of the one-armed man. It was night when they raided the still, and Mike grabbed one of the moonshiners and attempted to handcuff him. He knocked the moonshiner to the ground, forced one of his arms behind his back and attempted to grab the other arm to put it behind his back and place the cuffs on him. Having difficulty, Mike repeatedly demanded, "Give me the other arm". The moonshiner attempted to say something, but Mike told him to shut up and just give him the arm. This went on for a few seconds until the moonshiner was finally able to explain to Mike that he only had one arm.

In addition to moonshining, Cooley was involved in and had a record for armed robbery, safecracking, breaking and entering, and other violent crimes. In 1973, three individuals were found murdered in a Raleigh apartment. The three had been shot and were wrapped completely in duct tape. An investigation of the "Mummy Murders" conducted by the Raleigh Police Department and the SBI revealed that one of the victims was going to testify against Cooley in a robbery case. Cooley, according to witnesses, hired the shooter to kill the witness to prevent him from testifying, and the other two were killed because they were there and witnessed the killing. Cooley was named in a grand jury indictment as an unindicted co-conspirator, but was never charged. The actual shooter was tried and convicted for the murders.

In May 1977, Agent Bob Graham and I opened an investigation after receiving information that Cooley, a convicted felon, was carrying and using a firearm during crimes of violence. We developed enough information to get a federal search warrant for Cooley and his car. Through informant information and surveillance, we determined that he was spending a lot of time at the Foxy Lady, a strip joint in Raleigh.

We decided to execute the search warrant one afternoon as he came out of the club to get into his car, feeling that he would have a gun on him or if not certainly in the car. We approached him as he got to the car and executed the warrant. No gun was found on his person or the car. From the outset, he was calm and pleasant and did not appear nervous or worried at all, and I think Bob and I both realized there would be no gun.

After not finding anything, Bob commented to CV that he was surprised that he didn't have a gun, given his reputation for violence and robbing and crossing others along the way. He replied that if someone needed killing, he would not do it himself but have someone to do it for him.

Cooley was later arrested and convicted in state court for armed robbery and convicted in Federal courts for cocaine trafficking. He was sentenced to life in prison on the federal charges and died in prison in August 2017 at the age of 84. He was buried near his homeplace in the Oak Grove Baptist Church Cemetery, Youngsville, North Carolina.

Chapter Seven

BIRTH OF THE BUREAU
(1972)

The year 1972 would be a pivotal year for ATF and a very busy one for the Charlotte Division — and me in particular. In July, the long-awaited and much talked about reorganization of ATF took effect. ATF became a Bureau within the U.S. Treasury Department and no longer was a division of the IRS. Many hailed the move as a great day for ATF, no longer the "redheaded stepchild of the IRS" but an independent agency. Some, however, perhaps with a little more insight, warned of what might happen when the Washington crowd eventually took control. In any event, it happened and not only changed the structure of ATF, but also changed the direction and priorities, and over time the very culture of the agency. Some felt that the new agency should have a new name and solicited suggestions from the field. Several names were considered, but in the end it was decided to keep the name Alcohol, Tobacco and Firearms and just put Bureau in front. So we became the Bureau of Alcohol, Tobacco and Firearms (BATF). And some guy got an award for the new name.

Although Bureau Headquarters in Washington was now in charge, the regional structures remained in place (for the time being). Rex Davis was named the first Director of the new ATF, and John West was named the Deputy Director. It was rumored that ARC Bill Griffin was offered the job of Director of the new Bureau but declined because he did not want to move to Washington.

The National Gun Tracing Center was established in late 1972 to assist federal, state and local law enforcement agencies in solving crimes involving firearms. Firearms were traced from the manufacturer or importer to the purchaser from a licensed dealer. The tracing center expanded over the years and now traces most all firearms used in crimes and/or comes into the possession of law enforcement throughout the country.

ATF got its first female agent in June when Jo Ann Kocher was sworn in as an ATF Special Agent in New York.

The Assistant Regional Commissioners became Regional Directors (RD), the Special Investigators in Charge became Special Agents in Charge (SAC), Assistant Special Investigators in Charge became Assistant Special Agents in Charge (ASAC), and the Investigators in Charge to Resident Agent in Charge (RAC). The Area Supervisor and Regional Special Investigator positions were eliminated. Initially, there was little change as far as the field agents were concerned. Investigators were issued new credentials and badges with the new name, and their title changed from Special Investigator to Special Agent (SA).

However, things were indeed changing, and it would soon become obvious that Washington was calling the shots and the regional structure was eventually going to be eliminated altogether. While the Southeast Region was no longer calling the shots, it did remain very influential in determining how things happened. First of all, distillery and alcohol cases were still the primary measuring stick to determine how well ATF was doing its job, and, of course, the vast majority of cases were being made in the Southeast Region. Secondly, and over the long run more importantly and lasting, Southeast Region managers were being moved into key management positions in Washington as well as the other Regions. In fact, the office of Assistant Director for Criminal Enforcement was headed by former Southeast Region people through the 1970s and well into the late 1980s.

In October, the Charlotte District held a two-day statewide enforcement conference in Winston-Salem at the brand new Schlitz Brewery. The primary focus of the conference was the reorganization that had taken place in July and, more importantly, what the effect would be on the agent in the field. Newly appointed Charlotte SAC Bill Behen and representatives from the Regional office, including Assistant Regional Director Marvin Shaw, attended the conference. Our host treated us well including a guided tour of the facility with some free samples, as I recall. After some thought and reflection, it was later decided that perhaps there may be some perceived conflict of interest in being too cozy with an industry that we—"ATF"—regulated. We never went back.

By 1972 the buildup of personnel in the district and at Raleigh was pretty much completed. The Raleigh POD was up to about fifteen agents. Tommy Stokes transferred out to Alabama and was replaced by Chuck Stanfill from Atlanta. John Spidell transferred to Salisbury. We were still having a lot of liquor activity and of course, the firearms and explosives stuff remained primarily a compliance function rather than an enforcement matter. However, it was still time-consuming and took us away from our real job. It should be pointed out that not all viewed the firearms and explosives work in the same way. Some I recall with a little more foresight warned that liquor was dying and would soon be dead and we had better get with the new program or be left behind. And of course they were right, but just not yet. We still had a few more years we hoped (as it turned out, about four).

Franklin County Saturation

In January, a walk-through or saturation was conducted in Franklin County for one week. A walk through is when you bring in several agents to a particular location, in this case Franklin County, and literally walk through, drive-through, or fly over pretty much all of the county trying to locate distilleries. It is an attempt to validate or check on the estimated liquor distilleries (ATLIDS) in that particular location. The effort is to try to determine how many stills there are and not necessarily make arrests. Investigators are assigned in pairs and given an assigned area within the county, and literally walk through or drive through their area checking behind ever house, every little path into the woods, and any other place that might conceal a distillery. Investigators are brought in from other POD's to assist, and there were probably fifteen to twenty teams plus a Navy helicopter and ATF airplane. Six or eight stills were found and destroyed during the week, two of which were up and running and operating at the time of discovery.

The first was a large distillery in the Royal section of Franklin County just off US 401 south of Louisburg. Investigators Calcote and Bowen drove in on the still (four 720-gallon metal vats) in full operation. After lengthy foot chases, they caught and arrested Coy Jr. Pleasants and Bud Lowery (yes, again).

The second still in operation was located in the Youngsville section of Franklin County just off US-1 south of Franklinton. Investigator Tommy Stokes and I drove in behind an old abandoned house and noticed some light driving traffic going from the back of the house towards a small stand of pine trees. As luck would have it, we got the car stuck and spent five to ten minutes getting the car loose. Afterwards we continued to the wooded area and found a distillery (that appeared to be brand new) mashed in with the burners running. The distillery, which had been in full operation, consisted of two 500-gallon sub stills and several barrels. As in most cases, we blew the still up with dynamite or TNT. Tommy had the idea that perhaps we should also blow up the pump that was located in a small creek just down from this still. We did and in so doing set the woods on fire and spent the next 30 to 45 minutes putting out the fire (a valuable lesson learned).

A number of the investigators brought in for the saturation were older investigators who had at times in the past worked in Franklin and the surrounding counties. They remembered some of the old moonshiners from their previous time working there, and not surprisingly, it turned out some of the old moonshiners remembered them.

One night in particular, we were all at a local restaurant eating dinner and having a few beers when all of a sudden we learned that some of the patrons were the old bootleggers that the agents had worked in the past. A number of them got together talking about old times. The revenuers boasting, "Yes, I remember catching you at a still at such and such a location…," and the old moonshiners saying, "Well, that may be true but I remember operating that still on US 401 just south of Louisburg for over a year and watching you guys drive by two or three times a week passing just a few yards away and never knowing." Everybody had a laugh or two and it was quite a sight watching these one-time adversaries in the past now having a beer together and talking and laughing about the old times.

Rougemont Still

In February, we received information that Major Violator Reed Poole had a large still in the Rougemont area of Durham County. As the reported still was near the Orange, Durham, and Granville county lines, a rather large contingency of officers joined the search party.

Durham County ABC officers Charles Turner and Roland Leary, Orange County ABC officers Paul Cook and Burch Compton, Granville County ABC Chief Arthur Ray Currin, and Agent Devaney and I dropped off into the woods to find the still. We found the still deep in the woods on the first day. It was a steamer with two 55-gallon tank stills and mashed in with 2,200 gallons of mash. Since it appeared ready to run, we decided to stay in there and await the moonshiners. It was bitterly cold, and we found a sunny spot in a field close to the still to set up and wait.

On the second day we were all huddled in our observation bags and apparently had dozed off without noticing that an old black man and his dog had stumbled into and out of our encampment. Before any of us could react, he walked away, but it was obvious he had seen us and undoubtedly, we thought, would tell Poole or someone else and the word would get to Poole.

With no activity the next day, most of us felt that the still was hot (moonshiners knew or suspected it had been found and would not return) and we should just go ahead and blow it up. But Don, always the contrarian, said, "No, let's wait another day." And sure enough, the following morning at 4:00 am we heard the sound of a truck coming toward the still. The truck—loaded with plastic jugs, 100 lb bags of coal and 2,400 lbs of sugar—backed into the still yard and two individuals got out and were arrested. One of the moonshiners was Harold Poole, the brother of the Major Violator.

The still had no doubt been there a long time as we found one boiler completely burned out and mounds of coal ash on the ground. But in keeping with custom, we estimated that the still had been operating for a lesser period, in this case sixty days. The lesser estimated period of operation was actually a benefit to the moonshiner because the moonshiners could be taxed on the actual liquor seized as well as the estimated amount produced during the existence of the still.

In all seizures a mash sample was taken and sent to the lab to determine the alcoholic content, which is usually about 10%. Based on how long the still was in operation, the number of runs made during that period, and the alcohol content of the mash, an estimate was made as to how much liquor was made and how much the moonshiner owed in taxes at $10.50 per gallon. Not only would it be a little embarrassing to say it operated undetected for a year or more, quite honesty, it would be very difficult to prove that a distillery actually operated for a year or more.

Tampa Undercover

In March, for reasons still unknown to me, I was sent to Tampa, Florida to work an undercover case for the agents there. When my plane arrived, Investigators Warren Hilton and Larry Burkhalter met me and filled me in on the details of the case. There was a licensed gun dealer in the Sarasota area who was reportedly selling guns to straw purchasers, that is to someone other than the person who received the gun.

I went to the dealer and attempted to buy a pistol. He refused to sell me the gun because I was not a Florida resident, but told me if I could bring somebody in with a Florida license who was twenty-one years old he would sell me the gun using his name. A year later, I was subpoenaed to return and testify in the case that had been made against the dealer. My wife and the POD clerk Betty Haley, who were close friends, went with me to Florida for the trial. We were there for almost a week as the case kept getting delayed for one reason or another.

Hog-House Still

In March, we located a large still in a hog house near Bunn. The still was found as a result of a citizen telling Sheriff Dement that he was driving by early one morning before daylight and observed a truck coming from the barn with no lights on. We raided the still with a search warrant and arrested three men operating he still, one of which was a former major violator and another a well-known steam still operator. The distillery consisted of two 1,000-gallon tank stills, 9,000 gallons of mash, and 70 gallons of nontax paid whiskey that they had just made. It was one of the few "steam stills" we ever saw in Franklin County.

Salisbury Undercover

In April, I was asked to report to the Salisbury ATF office for an undercover assignment. I met with SI John Spidell (who had just transferred there from Raleigh), SI Bruce Bassett, and RAC

Bob Martin who had a source, Ray, who could introduce me to some liquor people in the Stanley, Montgomery, and Randolph counties area. There were no specific targets; the plan was just to be seen around some places and let it be known we were interested in buying some liquor. Over a period of two months, we purchased moonshine from four or five bootleggers, and also bought a couple of firearms. The largest buy was twenty cases (120 gals) from Paul and Buddy Brady in Asheboro.

Ironically, the Brady brothers were not known bootleggers to the Salisbury investigators. Initial contact was made with them though Elroy King, and old-time bootlegger who happened to be out of the business at that time (according to him). Ray and I went to his house in the Black Ankle section of Montgomery County. The area had a notorious reputation as being mountainous, clannish type people who were suspicious and unwelcoming of strangers, and a place where strangers should stay away from especially after dark. Even as a kid growing up in nearby Chatham County, I had heard tales about Black Ankle and how mean and rough the people were. Some stories even told of strangers going there and never being seen again. Real scary stuff to a young kid and no doubt exaggerated, but still a place you would avoid.

Anyway, we told Elroy we wanted to buy some whiskey and he said he had gotten out of the business, but he might be able to help us. He said he had a jar of good moonshine down at the spring and invited us down there to talk about things. He introduced us to "Uncle Buck" and told him to come along too and to bring his rifle "in case we run across some varmints that might needed shooting".

After sitting and talking for an hour or so and drinking most, if not all the jar, (it was obvious he was feeling us out to seeing if we would actually drink the moonshine and, if so, might have a lose tongue), Elroy said he could probably help us. He made a call and hooked me up with Buddy Brady, who I met in Asheboro and ordered ten cases of liquor. It was delivered a couple of days later by Paul Brady, who told me he had brought it from Wilkes County. We paid $35.00 a case, which was pretty cheap at that time.

The delivery was supposed to be made at 2:00 am in the morning at Elroy's house, but Brady never showed up. As I waited there alone in my car at 2:00 am in the morning, it crossed my mind,

"Boy, you are out here all alone in Black Ankle, they could kill you and take the money and probably no one would ever know what happened." I wasn't really scared, but was on super alert and really attentive to every sound or movement. Suddenly, I saw movement inside one of the old junked cars in the yard. It looked like someone had suddenly raised up and went back down in the backseat. A few minutes later it happened again and I could see it was Uncle Buck. He later told me that he slept in the cars at night because there was "so damn many dogs sleeping in the house there was no place for him to sleep."

A few days later I met the Brady's at the Sherwood Restaurant in Asheboro and ordered ten more cases. I was sitting in the back seat and the two of them were in the front seat as we talked about arrangements for the buy. All of a sudden Douglas turned and looked at me and said, "You are the law you little son-of-bitch and I know it." I thought, "Where did that come from?" and more importantly, "What am I going to say?" As I pondered, the thought of my Smith and Wesson 5-shot revolver in my pocket offered some assurance. Then I said, "Well, if I am the law, you are already caught so you might as well sell me the ten cases and use the money to pay your lawyer." For a few seconds nothing happened, and then he laughed and said, "You are all right, boy," and I started to breathe again. We later set up a knock-off buy (order a large quantity of moonshine and pay with the badge when delivered) and the two were arrested by Agent Spidell when they made the delivery.

Big Still in Merry Hill

In May, ATF agents and local officers raided a mega distillery operation in the Merry Hill section of Bertie County. The still consisted of four 4500-gallon tank stills with a 500-gallon high pressure boiler enclosed in an add-on building behind a mobile home. The still was located primarily through the work of Regional Special Agent Phil McGuire as part of undercover and raw materials investigation in Tennessee.

Evidence gathered showed that the still had operated almost two years and had manufactured over 153,000 gallons of illicit liquor. The still was put up and owned by a group of bootleggers from Tennessee and North Carolina, including Major Violator Lonless Fields of Durham. Fields and six others were indicted and tried in U.S. Eastern District Court in Washington, North Carolina, in October 1973. Six of the seven including Fields were found guilty and sentenced to serve time in federal prison. Fields was sentenced to a term of five years in prison and fined $5,000. All filed a Notice of Appeal.

Subsequent to the convictions, I was talking to an informant in Granville County and the subject of the Merry Hill case came up and the prison sentence for Lonless Fields. The informant kind of chuckled and said Fields would get out of it and wouldn't go to prison. I pointed out to him that this was a Federal Court case and not some little local county court. He went on to say that the fix was in, that $50,000 had been delivered to some fat lawyer in Rocky Mount who would take care of things. Several months later Federal Judge John Larkins suspended the active sentence for Fields and the others and placed them on probation.

The Merry Hill distillery was very similar to a large still seized in Cabarrus County in March of 1968. The Cabarrus distillery consisted of twelve 1082-gallon metal tank stills whereas the Merry Hill distillery had four 4500-gallon stills. Other than the number and sizes of the stills, the two setups were almost identical in terms of design, construction, and operation.

The Cabarrus still was underground and concealed by an old barn and could only be accessed from inside the barn. According to ATF Supervisor Bob Martin, it was concealed to the point that a search of the area earlier failed to turn up any clues that the massive distillery was there. The Merry Hill still, contained in the mobile home add-on room, was concealed from view by the mobile home. According to Martin, the Cabarrus still may have been in operation for up to ten years. The Merry Hill still was estimated to have operated between eighteen months and two years. Martin said there was no doubt in his mind that both stills were designed, engineered and constructed by the same man, and he had a pretty good idea who but he could not prove it.

Drop-off Man Finds Still

The common practice when looking for a still in a particular area (usually in the woods) is for a number of officers to go into the woods to search. They go by vehicle to the vicinity of the area to be searched, get out of the vehicle, and quickly get into the woods hopefully without being seen. The driver of the vehicle is the drop-off man and he departs the area after making the drop. Depending on how long the officers might be in the woods, he might stay in the area to make the pickup after an hour or so. Or, in the case where the officers might be watching a still for days, he might leave the area and make periodic checks (remember no cell phones and radios with limited range that may or may not work). In most situations, the drop-off man is removed from and not a part of the action (finding and/or raiding the still).

An exception occurred in June when information was received that there was a large still located in the Royal section of Franklin County. Mr. Zetts dropped Supervisor Steely, Agent Stanfill, and me off in the woods to check out the information. After walking several miles, we came upon a vehicle parked in the woods and discovered it was Mike. He said, "What took you so long? The still is about 200 yards over there."

After dropping us off, he had randomly parked in the woods behind a church where people were driving in and dumping garbage, and had gotten out and walked around and just came upon the still. We later arrested two moonshiners and destroyed the two 900-gallon sub stills and 1,700 gallons of mash. As far as I know, it was the only time the drop-off man actually found a still.

I Couldn't Shoot Him

In June, we located a distillery in the White Level area of Franklin County. It was a small still but memorable to me because it was the first time the senior agents let me be the flush man, and it didn't go as planned. The flush man, as previously noted, is the officer that approaches the still and tries to get close enough to catch a violator prior to them running from the still, where they are presumably caught by the other officers surrounding the still.

As I snuck down the still path, I could see a man with his back to me stirring a barrel of mash with a long wooden pole. As I got just about close enough to grab him, he had turned and was facing me. He saw me and withdrew the pole (maybe 6 ft long and 2" in diameter) from the barrel and drew it back as if to strike me. The mash barrel was between him and me so I stopped of course, and told him to drop it. He did not and drew it back farther. After telling him a couple times to drop it and him not doing so, I drew my pistol and again said drop it and again he didn't. Well, it was one of those times when you think, "What do I do now"? I knew I could not just shoot him, nor was I going to try to get any closer as long as he had the pole drawn back in such a threatening manner. I'm thinking surely another officer will come to my aid.

After what seemed like ten or fifteen minutes (probably no more than a minute) the man dropped the pole and I handcuffed him. At that same moment, I could hear loud laughter off to my side. The other guys had observed what became known as "the stand-off at White Level" and were rolling on the ground with laughter. The other still hand got away and they never even tried to catch him because they were too interested in watching and laughing at me. The old man apologized profusely, saying he was not going to hit me, but was so scared he just froze and really could not do anything for that brief period. I believed him because, while maybe not scared, for a minute I wasn't sure what to do myself.

First Firearms Case

As still seizures continued to decline, we were all encouraged to start working firearms investigations. In July, I wrote my first firearms criminal case in Durham. Leonard B. was arrested and charged with violations of the GCA of 1968, specifically being a felon in possession of a sawed-off firearm and falsifying the ATF form 4473 in connection with the purchase. While still somewhat hesitant to take firearms cases, the US Attorney Office in the Middle District accepted and prosecuted the case. Generally, neither we, nor the US Attorney were too concerned about simple firearms violations. Possession of a sawed-off shotgun with no violence or intended violence and a one-time convicted felon possessing a firearm with no indication of intended violence were just not pursued. In the case of the sawed-off shotgun, the possessor was given the option of abandoning the weapon and we would destroy it.

Bobby Marshall Shooting

In September, a walk-through or saturation was conducted in Robeson County. Unlike the Franklin County saturation done to

identified and asked to voluntarily comply and stop selling sugar and jars to moonshiners. Well that is not quite true, they were first told they could continue to sell as long as they let us know who, when, and where the materials would be delivered or picked up. Very few chose to do that. Those who continued to sell could be issued a "Demand Letter", which required monthly reports to ATF on all disposition of sugar and/or jars.

In the Raleigh area, "Demand Letters" were issued to Keith Store on Hwy 98 west of Wake Forest and Food Fair Grocery in Henderson. When approached about the sale of sugar and jars, Mr. Keith insisted he sold only to ladies for use in canning fruits and vegetables. After a quick calculation it was determined that if that was true, the good ladies of Wake Forest canned enough fruit and vegetable to feed about half the state. Later on the moonshiners started using one gallon plastic jugs instead of the glass jars. And right there in Wake Forest was Neuse Plastics, which made and sold one-gallon plastic jugs (milk containers). The plastic containers were found at several stills, but to my knowledge none were ever traced directly to the company.

The Harricanes

"I am looking for James Perry. Do you know where he lives?
"Yeah, he lives over yonder in the harricanes."
"Well, where is the harricanes?"
"Well, it starts over yonder (pointing to the east) and goes to over yonder (pointing to the west)".

The best I can tell, there is a large section of land in northern Wake County and southern Granville and Franklin County known as the harricanes, or as the locals say "hair-kins" or "har-a-kins". Dating back to the Depression era, it was considered a pretty desolate run-down land and its inhabitants were very poor and looked down upon as somewhat low class. According to some, it got its name from a massive hurricane that came through in the early 1900s and destroyed everything standing.

The land was pretty much rocky or red clay and not suitable for crops. To make a living, a lot of the people turned to making liquor and it quickly became known for its good moonshine. Depending on whom you talk to, the harricanes starts over toward Zebulon and follows NC 96 and NC 98 west to around Creedmoor. Some say its south boundary is the Neuse River in Wake County and its north boundary is Franklinton. Others disagree.

Today, only a few of the old timers know the history of the har-ricanes and talk of how it was back then. With the tremendous growth over the past few decades in Wake County and Raleigh, the useless, worthless piece of ground has now become very valu-able and is filled with large sprawling subdivisions and expensive homes.

Dunn POD

Dunn was a small post of duty with a supervisor (Bob Furr) and three investigators (Ronnie Williams, Hoyt Lumpkin and John Lorrick), but had one of the most prolific liquor counties in the state that being Johnston County. Dunn agents worked closely with Johnston County ABC officers James Barefoot and Guy Lee but were still often short-handed and regularly called upon Raleigh agents for assistance in raiding stills.

In working liquor, as in most areas of law enforcement, there is a lot of down time and waiting. Waiting for the weather, waiting for the informant to call, waiting for the moonshiners to move, waiting for darkness, waiting for the search warrant, etc. Back in those days of just waiting, often when four or more officers came together, a poker game would break out (just to kill some time of course). And in looking back, I must say Johnston County seemed to have had a lot of "waiting days" especially when Raleigh and Dunn investigators got together.

On one occasion we were called on to help on a surveillance of a large still located just off Highway 70, west of Selma. The still had been dismantled and, according to an informant, was going to be moved to a new site within the next two or three days. A rather large contingency of agents from Raleigh, Dunn and Fayetteville, assembled at the Holiday Inn in Selma to plan and conduct the surveillance. We would take turns on the ground watching the still and the remaining agents would stage in the motel waiting for the movement to start and then follow. And with nothing to do but wait, of course a poker game broke out at the motel. On the second night, an excited young Dunn agent (John Lorrick) came running into the room shouting Bob (Furr) they are getting ready to move, we have got to go now. "To hell with that still, somebody deal, I'm $150 loser," said Bob. "We will find it later" and true to his word, they did locate and destroy it a couple months later.

Another time, Agent Stanfill and I were sent to help raid a large still in Johnston County. The distillery, consisting of about twenty-five mashed-in submarine stills, was located in a wooded area fenced off from a much larger fenced-in area containing a large number of pigs. After the raid and arrest of the moonshiners, we destroyed the still by use of explosives. When the stills blew, the nearly 8,000 gallons of mash went everywhere, settling in a small stream and several low places in the pigpen. The pigs, of course, quickly slopped up the mash and in a short time they started staggering and falling down— the pigs were drunk. A local TV station came out and filmed the "drunk hogs" story and it made the evening news.

Chapter Eight
THE FADING MOONSHINE (1973-1974)

Nationally, the ATF reorganization continued to move forward. Headquarters and Regional senior management positions continued to be filled by southeast regional personnel. William (Tommy) Thompson was appointed Deputy Director replacing John West, who retired and moved back to NC. John Corbin was named the Assistant Director for Criminal Enforcement. Jarvis Brewer was named Assistant Director for Internal Affairs. Marvin Shaw was named Mid-Atlantic Regional Director, and M.L. Goodwin was named Assistant Director for the North Atlantic Region (NY).

Locally, the primary focus was still on liquor enforcement, although more and more time was being spent on firearms and explosives. The firearms and explosives regulatory effort continued and we were starting to pay more attention to criminal violations of the GCA of 1968. As noted above, the U.S. Attorneys were starting to take and prosecute selective firearms cases.

Big Tennessee Still

In March, a large distillery was located in Jefferson County, Tennessee. The distillery was reportedly partially owned by Major Violators in North Carolina—including Lonless Fields—and much of the liquor was coming to Durham and other areas of North Carolina. As a result it was decided that Knoxville agents would set up a surveillance on the still and we (NC agents) would attempt to follow the liquor from the still to see where and to whom it was going in the state. Agent Stanfill and I were assigned to the investigation as were Charlie Mercer of the Wilkesboro POD, and RAC Bob Martin of the Salisbury POD. SA/Pilot Marshall Reece was assigned to provide aerial support. We set up at the Lemon Tree Inn/Aunt Sarah's Pancake House on I-40 near Marion, North

Carolina. The plan was that we would be notified when a liquor transporter left the still and we would pick him up on I-40 and follow him to the delivery point. We followed one pick up all the way to Edenton, North Carolina, resulting in the seizure of 600 gallons of NTPW by local agents and officers.

As is the case with a lot of well-planned things, things don't always go as planned. Only one additional vehicle left from the still over the period of about a month coming our way. I heard the operators were having troubles with the still because of its size and sophistication. The distillery was subsequently raided and the violators were arrested. It was described as "the largest illicit still-fermenter in ATF history". It consisted of one large metal tank with a mash capacity of 15,227 gallons. The still had twelve electric motors to stir the mash and was operated by steam boiler. The still was constructed underground and then a large barn was built over the still with conveyers to carry raw materials down to the still and to bring the finished whiskey up. Although the results were less than anticipated, I learned to play hearts, heard a lot of "war stories", and ate a lot of pancakes.

Sand Bagger

SA Stanfill and I were pretty much working partners and we played a lot of golf, as a great deal of our work was at night. We actually found a submarine still on the Cheviot Hills golf course in Raleigh in a wooded area between the third and fourth fairways (no doubt while looking for a lost ball). We sometimes checked the still two or three times a week, but it was never mashed in. In June, SA Stanfill talked me into going to Georgia with him to play golf in the fourth annual "Brack Poe Open". The get-together was started by ATF employees in Georgia and had become an event over the years. I agreed to go and submitted my handicap scores. As it turned out, he won the Third Flight and I won the Second Flight. Of course, "sandbaggers" was the response to our winning.

I returned to the tournament a number of succeeding years, but never came close to winning again. Just "beginners luck" I suppose. I enjoyed and looked forward each year to meeting and fellowshipping with agents from all over the southeast.

Garland Bunting

Garland Bunting was an ABC Officer in Halifax County who was known throughout the area for his skills, accomplishments and stories in pursuing moonshiners. Although a county officer, he loved working with ATF and became very good friends with the agents in Rocky Mount, Raleigh, and elsewhere. Garland was quite a storyteller and told many stories of his experiences working undercover, posing as a fish peddler, saw mill operator, etc.

Dennis Rogers wrote a piece about Garland's exploits in the *Raleigh News and Observer* in the early 1980s. In 1985, Alec Wilkinson, a writer for *New Yorker* magazine wrote a story about him and later a book called *Moonshine: A Pursuit of White Liquor*. The author wrote how he enjoyed the many stories and commented that he "became drunk on Garland's stories". The book led to Garland appearing on the David Letterman Show and three small movie rolls. I remember sitting in a hotel in New York City waiting to start my shift on a United Nations Detail, when I heard the announcer say tonight's guests include Garland Bunting, and of course I watched his segment. He appeared in the Kevin Costner film Bull Durham (1988), the Paul Newman movie Blaze (1989), and the Vernon Jones Story in 1994.

Despite his many successes and fame, Garland remained a very folksy, jovial, humble, down to earth man. Perhaps the only exception to his demeanor was when his young son was killed in a tragic accident in Raleigh. Garland and his family had come to Raleigh to attend a going away dinner for Agent Joe Kopka, who was transferring to Headquarters. Garland had known and worked with Joe a long time going back to when Joe was stationed in Rocky Mount and Elizabeth City. Garland and his family were staying with Mike, and while they were at the dinner the boys were riding their bikes and Garland's son hit the curb and fell off, hitting his head. I recall that they took the boy to the hospital to be checked and he seemed to be okay, so they came back to Mike's house. The boy died a day or so later and Garland took it extremely hard; some say he never got over it.

I last saw Garland in 1993 when we invited him to attend a joint firearms qualification (Greensboro and Raleigh offices) in Chatham County. He seemed the same old Garland and told some of the same old stories that I had heard many times before. The new agents, who had never worked liquor and known Garland, were pleasant and laughed politely, but I remember thinking that they really didn't get it and could not appreciate who he was and what he had seen and done as a revenuer. Garland passed away in 1995 after suffering a heart attack.

Wilkesboro POD

Wilkesboro and the Wilkes County area were known as the "Moonshine Capital" in the 1950s and '60s. It was where Jr. Johnson and other NASCAR racers learned to drive while transporting moonshine and trying to outrun revenuers. The ATF office was located in the basement of the federal building in Wilkesboro.

In 1968, investigator Bob Powell transferred to Wilkesboro as the Investigator in Charge. Shortly thereafter, several new investigators were assigned to the Wilkesboro office. Powell's management style was somewhat militaristic, setting up two squads each competing against each other. To promote the competitive spirit and the necessity of physical fitness, he started the "Wilkesboro Olympics", where agents were required to participate in five events: the 100-yard dash, the mile run, pistol shooting, the mattock throw, and barrel cutting. Based on his outstanding performance and "contribution to the community", Bob was presented the Southeast Region Special Agent of the Year Award by Regional Director Griffin in 1973. Sadly, later that year Bob's son, Steve, was killed in an automobile accident.

Many agents throughout the Charlotte District got their training and experience working moonshine while stationed in Wilkesboro. One who stayed in Wilkesboro was Sam Cabe, also known as "Old Blue". At first appearance, Sam looked more like a mountain moonshiner than an agent. He was a cagey old guy who knew the mountains and moonshiners more than anyone.

Sam was very interesting to listen to as he talked about the old days and his undercover work throughout the District. Sam retired in 1973 after thirty-one years of working moonshine. Powell was transferred to Detroit, and most of the agents were transferred out when "liquor offices" were closed throughout the south in 1976. Only two agents remained, and they, too, were transferred out when the Wilkesboro ATF office closed for good in July 1980. Even the Wilkesboro federal building itself was eventually closed. In the heyday of moonshining, it was said that the Wilkesboro POD averaged at least one still-bust per day.

Firearms Cases

As still seizures continued to decline, more emphasis was placed on enforcement of the firearms laws. In addition to our continuing compliance responsibilities, attention was turned to the criminal violations under the GCA of 1968. The primary violations charged were in three areas: 1) felons and other prohibited persons buying or possessing firearms and making false statements to dealers regarding their prohibited status when making purchases; 2) persons possessing unregistered sawed-off shotguns and rifles, machine guns and destructives; and, 3) an occasional dealing without a federal firearms license. Although not charged early on, Section 924 C, carrying/using a firearm during a drug trafficking offense, would later be the most charged violation of the GCA of 1968.

Disbanding ATF

In 1974, rumors spread that the administration was planning to disband ATF and transfer its functions to various other agencies. ATF leadership denied that there was such a proposal or plan. The rumors, however, persisted to the point that the Secretary of the Treasury and later the ATF Director sent letters to employees debunking the rumors and assuring the employees no such action was planned.

The Explosives Taggant and Significant Criminal programs were introduced. Under the explosives taggant program, manufactures would be required to place minute chips or taggants in all explosives manufactured that would contain identifying information about the explosives. The thinking was that in the event of a bombing or explosion, the chips would provide the investigator with information as to the type and manufacturer of the explosives and a possible trace to the retail purchaser.

The Significant Program or Significant Criminal Enforcement Program – Armed and Dangerous, as it was officially named, was established to identify and prosecute significant armed criminals. Under the program, "ATF Special Agents will identify and then make cases against the Nation's most violent and dangerous criminals in communities all over the US," said ATF Director Davis. The program directed each ATF office to meet with local and state officers in their area to identify significant criminals (individuals who unlawfully acquires, possess, transports or otherwise uses or deals in firearms, explosives or destructive devices and who were currently and actively engaged in felonious criminal activity that represented a serious threat to the public safety). Each District was directed to contact local and state agencies to attempt to identify the worst of the criminals in their particular localities. They were then to prepare a roster of the identified major criminals using firearms in committing crimes and to attempt to develop criminal cases against them (sounds like the Major Liquor Violator List).

Moonshine arrests and seizures continued to decline in the North Carolina and the Southeast. North Carolina agents seized only 325 moonshine stills and made only 436 alcohol arrests in 1974, and less than half those numbers the following year. While the continuous decline in seizures and arrests could be attributed to strenuous enforcement efforts and the increasing availability of legal liquor, the cost of making moonshine also became a significant factor.

The price of sugar, the main purchased ingredient for making moonshine, skyrocketed in the mid 1970s because of embargos and a worldwide shortage and high demand for sugar. Sugar prices tripled and even quadrupled in some areas. The moonshiner went from paying $15.00 per hundred pounds to paying $45.00 or $60.00 for the same amount. To be profitable, he had to increase the price of his product to the point the moonshine versus legal liquor cost was no longer a significant difference and factor for the consumer.

Franklin County continued to be the most prolific area in terms of liquor seizures and arrests, with stills seizures in the Franklinton, Rocky Ford, Centerville, Louisburg, White Level and Youngsville areas. Typically the stills were small, usually two or three subs ranging in size from 280 gallons to 480 gallons.

Unique Tomb

William Andrew Jeffrey, a young attorney from a prominent Franklin County family, was elected to the North Carolina senate in 1844. A year later, he came down with the fever and died. It seems that Mr. Jeffrey had a fear of being buried in the ground where his body might be eaten by worms. The fear was such that he made his family promise that he would not be buried in the ground, but in a rock so the worms could not get to him.

His family honored his request and found a gigantic boulder, had it chiseled out, and entombed his body inside the boulder. The Unique Tomb is in the family cemetery located a few yards off US 401 near NC 98 in Franklin County. For many years there was a state historical marker on US 401 directing visitors to the tomb, but the marker was removed after vandals continuously damaged the tomb and other grave sites there.

There was a marble slab on top of the tomb with an inscription about Mr. Jeffrey. The slab was broken by vandals and later removed. I recall the inscription said something like, "he was a kind man, a loyal and honest man, an attorney and state senator, and a faithful public servant."

Upon reading the epitaph, one person speculated that there had to be at least two people buried inside the rock.

Cascine Plantation Still

In March, we discovered a large still south of Louisburg in the pre-revolutionary Cascine House, which sits on and was a part of an old plantation dating back to 1752. After conducting surveillance for a few days, we raided the still and arrested the two moonshiners running the still. The seizure consisted of two 480-gallon subs, thirty mash barrels and 108 gallons of moonshine. During the surveillance we were able to follow one of the moonshiners to a nearby mobile home. After destroying the still, we searched the mobile home and found 954 gallons of moonshine in the mobile home. When asked why they had such a large amount stockpiled, they said they were having a hard time finding buyers.

I-85 Still

In June, we located and subsequently seized a large distillery in Warren County, in a wooded area a few yards off Interstate 85 just below the Virginia line. The investigation was worked with Granville County ABC Officer Arthur Ray Currin and Warren County deputy sheriff Dorsey Capps, and was located through ground and aerial surveillance from Granville County. The seizure consisted of two 1800-gallon submarine stills, 2,000 gallons of mash, and related equipment. We arrested Nathaniel Davis and Bud Lowery (again), who were operating the still at the time of the raid.

Southeast Region Airborne Operations

In the mid-60s, the Southeast Region initiated and developed the use of aerial surveillance to assist in the anti-moonshine effort. Special Agent Charlie Weems, one of the developers of the program, became the first ATF pilot and later on the Chief of the Southeast Airborne Operations Section, which by the mid-1970s had seven pilots: Tommy Pritchett, Donald Watson, Linwood Hall, William Duke, William Ivey, Marshall Reece and Weems. We in North Carolina—and Raleigh in particular—were very fortunate to have Special Agent/Pilot Marshall Reece assigned to the Raleigh office.

Marshall was a "work alcoholic" and could always be counted on to help, often on short notice. If he were needed but unavailable, he would arrange to have another pilot come in to assist. I called on him many times, often in the wee hours of morning, to fly over a particular house or location to help me follow a still hand or raw materials transporter to locate their stills and stashes.

During the Wagering investigation conducted by the Raleigh POD in 1975, Marshall flew many hours helping to identify and track all the wagering participants. And during cigarette smuggling enforcement, Marshall was instrumental in long, over-the-road surveillances from North Carolina to West Virginia and New York City.

Family Fun Day

In May, the first (and only to my knowledge only) "Family Fun Day" was held in Salisbury for North Carolina employees and their spouses and children. The event was hosted by the Salisbury POD, and a delicious supper was prepared by RAC Bob Martin, SA John Spidell, and Asheville RAC Kolen Flack.

The highlight of the day was the long-anticipated grudge softball game between the Wilkesboro Olympians led by RAC Bob Powell, and the rest of the ATFers led by ASAC Jim Elder. Charlotte SAC Bill Behen and former Deputy Director John West were the umpires. The Rest of the ATFers jumped out to an early lead, but the Wilkesboro Olympians (obviously in better physical condition) came back to win 17 to 11.

Chapter Nine
THE WAGERING LAWS
(1975)

The new year ushered in significant changes both nationally, and locally as well. ATF was given a new jurisdiction and responsibility for enforcing the federal wagering laws. President Ford directed ATF to hire and train 500 new agents to be assigned to major metropolitan areas.

The Federal Law Enforcement Training Center (FLETC) at Glynco, Georgia was opened in the fall at the former Glynco Naval Air Station. The new training center consolidated and transferred all Treasury agency training from the Washington area to the new site near Brunswick, Georgia. ATF started training new agents shortly after the opening and the first New Agent Class graduated in February 1976. Atlanta ASAC Ed Hughes was initially delegated to be the "managing coordinator" for ATF training activities. In July 1976, Peter Mastin was appointed the first Chief of ATF Law Enforcement Training at Glynco. Under Mastin's leadership, new agent training was expanded and a number of advanced agent training programs were developed as well as training programs for state and local officer.

Charlotte SAC Bill Behen retired and ASAC Jim Elder was reassigned as the SAC of the St. Louis District. John Westra was appointed SAC and Steve Whitlow ASAC for the Charlotte District. Westra had been the ASAC in the Birmingham District and Whitlow came in from the Group Supervisor position in the Atlanta District. Locally, Mike Zetts resumed the RAC position in Raleigh after Herb Steely transferred to HQ.

Orange County Poker Houses

In February, Orange County ABC Officer Paul Cook contacted me about working undercover to expose gambling activity within the county. I met with him and Orange County Deputy Talbert, who advised that the Sheriff wanted the poker houses in the county closed down, and they asked me to do the undercover. They identified an individual named Jack who they thought was running the poker houses. I stopped by the gas station that he operated and talked with him about buying or leasing some land. He said he had the perfect place and asked if I wanted to go see it. I told him I did not have time, I had to get back home (Raleigh) because it was my poker night and didn't want to miss it. His eyes lit up and he said, "We have a little game around here if you are interested." I told him I might be and would talk with him about in a week or so when I got back over that way.

A few days later I did return and played in his poker house on the land he tried to sell me. Orange County gave me $300.00 to use in the investigation. I lost it all the first night in wild card game that I had never played or even heard of. That, of course, got me in tight with Jack — he had a sucker with money and was going to get all of it he could. Orange County, on the other hand, was not too thrilled when I informed them I had lost all the funds, as they had anticipated the $300 for the entire investigation.

After playing a few times at Jacks, I moved on to two or three other "poker houses" and played. My luck turned and I was able to about break-even, which made Orange County happy. Midway through the investigation, I was pulled out by the SAC as we were about to undertake the new Federal wagering law and he anticipated a possible conflict.

SBI Agent Vance Furr was brought in to replace me with some phony story I had to get out of town for a while. He went with me to a couple games and was able to move right in as another sucker with money. He and I must have appeared as a curious fit as I was maybe 140 lbs. and barely 5'7", and he well over was 6 feet and weighed 200 plus pounds. They successfully completed the investigation with search warrants and the arrest of thirty people.

Wagering Case

ATF was given the responsibility of enforcing the federal wagering laws when the jurisdiction was transferred from the IRS to ATF in December 1974. Wagering schools were quickly set up in each district to train agents in the law and enforcement methods. In the Charlotte District, the one-week class was held in Benson, North

Carolina in March. Instructors for the class were Lance Hearn, Dick Garner, Charlie Weems and Jim Bright from the Regional Counsels Office. The wagering law, like most ATF enforced laws, was actually a tax law. Under the wagering law, any person engaged in the wagering business must obtain a federal occupational tax stamp yearly ($500) and pay a monthly excise tax of 2% on gross income. The law related primarily to sports betting operations and lotteries or number games.

At the outset, each POD was instructed to gather information and intelligence as to the existence and scope of wagering activity within their area. I was given the assignment for the Raleigh POD. Through contacts with the Durham Police, it was determined that a significant lottery operation existed, and had so for many years. After the period of intelligence gathering, the SAC authorized two investigations to be conducted: the Durham lottery and a lottery operating within the Salisbury POD.

The Durham lottery was a numbers game where individuals picked and bet on a three-digit winning number. The winning number was determined by the daily activities of the New York Stock Exchange and published daily in the newspaper. In the financial section under the caption "What Stocks Did", the number of stocks advancing, declining, and remaining unchanged were listed. By taking the last digit of each number, the winning number was derived. Thusly, the winning number of the following example is 850:

<u>What Stocks Did</u>
ADVANCES: 36<u>8</u>
DECLINES: 16<u>5</u>
UNCHANGED: 91<u>0</u>

Primarily through information from the Durham PD, Michael Harris was identified as a major player in the Durham lottery. In April, Special Agent Stanfill and I started conducting surveillance of Harris in and around various neighborhoods in Durham. It quickly became evident that Harris was the pick-up man in the Durham area. He had an established route daily, going to various houses in the African-American neighborhoods and departing after a short period often carrying a brown paper bag. Subsequently, a

Special Employee (informant) was brought into the investigation and was able to make buys (purchase lottery tickets) in most of the identified houses visited by Harris.

With the assistance of aerial surveillance by Special Agent/Pilot Reece, and Agents Calcote and Garrison (Stanfill was transferred to HQ), we were able to follow Harris to the Hillsborough/Mebane area, where he met and handed over the tickets and money to a man later identified to be William G. of Snow Camp, North Carolina. Based on surveillance of William G. and his associates, and information from other sources, it was determined that he was the head of the organization and it went beyond Durham to Kinston, Goldsboro, Sanford, Alamance County, and other areas of the state. It was further determined that his base of operations was in a rented house near Mebane.

In August, federal search warrants were obtained and executed for the "count house" in Mebane, and twenty-five other residences and vehicles in Durham and Alamance County. William G. and two other individuals were at the "count house" at the time of the search, processing the day's numbers and monies.

The search of the residence disclosed evidence of a full-scale numbers operation with numerous wagering records and paraphernalia found. The execution of the search warrants resulted in the seizure of approximately $35,000 in cash and eight vehicles, and boxes of lottery records and paraphernalia. We also found evidence of a safety deposit box in a bank in Siler City and subsequently obtained a search warrant and opened the box. It contained thirty-three rubber bands and some money wrappers but no cash (we just missed).

As in most federal cases of this scale, it was decided that arrests would not be made in conjunction with the execution of the search warrants, but that evidence obtained during the searches, along with other evidence in the case would later be submitted to U.S. Attorney's Office for Grand Jury indictments.

After analysis of the records seized and all follow-up investigation, a criminal case report was submitted to the U.S. Attorney's Office, Middle District of North Carolina, recommending indictment and prosecution of nineteen individuals. No one was ever indicted, and to my knowledge no other action was ever taken relative to the case. Speculation was (and still is to my mind) no action was taken and the matter ultimately dismissed due to the fact that the newly appointed U.S. Attorney was from Durham and felt it would be politically unwise to pursue the matter. The individuals were assessed civilly for the estimated taxes due, including William G., the owner.

As to whether or not they were collected I do not know. I understand at least one additional investigation met a similar fate. In New York City, I was told, a lottery investigation was shut down because it was having an adverse impact on the local economy of the area. After a year, the wagering laws were transferred back to the IRS, where to my knowledge no more criminal investigations were conducted. After all, the real intent of the law was to collect taxes — not to conduct and perfect criminal cases. Someone apparently failed to understand, ATF Criminal Enforcement was in the law enforcement and putting people in jail business, not the tax assessment and collection business.

In September, SA Garrison and I were having lunch (a world-famous cheeseburger, I am sure) at Johnsons Restaurant in Siler City, when we observed a 1972 Plymouth pass by on US 64. We recognized the car as being one for which we had a search and seizure warrant issued that was not found during August searches. We followed the vehicle and subsequently pulled it over. William G. was operating the vehicle and before we could get to him he announced, "I have my tax license and my lawyer said you couldn't arrest me."

I told him that was fine, but we had a warrant to seize the vehicle and were going to do so. He objected initially, but later said okay and asked if he could remove his personal stuff from the car. We told him he could, at which time he opened and removed three or four large sacks. We had no doubt that the bags were full of lottery tickets and money, but had no choice but to let him go. His attorney had already complained to the US Attorney's Office about us continuing to harass him even after he got his tax stamp, and of course the cease and desist order had been passed on to us.

While the wagering investigation consumed a great deal of time during the year, we were starting to make more gun cases and a few liquor cases. In September, Winston-Salem and Wilkesboro agents seized and destroyed a large still in Pleasant Garden near Greensboro. The still had a mash capacity of 18,000 gallons and was said to be producing 670 gallons of moonshine daily.

Chapter Ten

DRASTIC CHANGES
(1976)

D uring 1976, drastic changes were in the making for ATF, especially affecting the Southeast Region. Unknown to most at the time, the perfect storm was developing, one that would bring about a devastating effect on the personnel in the Southeast Region and Charlotte Division, and signal the end to federal moonshining enforcement. The Director announced two major initiatives: a new Reorganization Plan and Project CUE (Concentrated Urban Enforcement). Both would bring significant changes nationally, and to the Southeast Region and Charlotte District the changes would be drastic.

Criminal Enforcement Reorganization

Under the announced Criminal Enforcement Reorganization, the Office of Criminal Enforcement in Headquarters would be realigned with three divisions: 1) Program Development and Planning, 2) Program Review, and 3) Investigations. The most significant change and the real reason for the reorganization—Regional Offices would be removed from the organizational structure. The Regional Directors and the Asst. Regional Directors, along with their respective staffs, would be eliminated. SACs would report directly to the Assistant Director-Criminal Enforcement (ADCE) in Washington. Regulatory Enforcement organization was virtually unchanged, retaining the existing regional and field structure. Laboratory services, regional counsel, and certain other functions would also remain in the regions.

In his announcement Director Davis said, "It should be made absolutely clear to all persons with whom this matter was discussed, that no further change in the ATF organizational structure is contemplated. In particular, there is no intention to alter in any way the regulatory function at the regional level, nor to transfer any regulatory authority from the regional level to the national level."

You would have to be blind not to see, I think, this "One Bureau" concept was directed primarily at the Southeast Region. While the changes would have a major effect at the higher echelon, it appeared at the time to have little effect on the day-to-day work of the agent in the field. The reorganization was approved and eventually implemented resulting in the elimination of the Regional Directors and their staff. Southeast Regional Director Bill Griffin would retire bringing an end to an era.

Project CUE (Concentrated Urban Enforcement)

The second major initiative announced by the Director was Project CUE, a program designed to curb the criminal misuse of firearms and explosives and armed violence and street crimes. The program was to be implemented in the major metropolitan areas where the increase in violent gun crimes was increasing at an alarming rate. Washington, Boston, and Chicago were the initial three cities selected for the implementation of the program. Under the plan, additional ATF agents would be sent to these areas to concentrate on reducing the gun violence. The plan called for a mix of experienced agents and newly hired agents who would work in conjunction with various state and local agencies to address the problem.

By 1976, the moonshine problem in the south had been reduced significantly and while not totally eliminated was obviously dying out. Liquor arrests and seizure were down significantly across the south. Firearms and explosives cases, on the other hand, were on the increase. Most of the firearms and explosives cases were being made in the larger urban areas where the violent crime and misuse of firearms and explosives was occurring.

So, on the one hand there was a need for Special Agents in the large metropolitan areas (CUE cities), and at the same time you had large numbers of Special Agents assigned to small rural "liquor offices" with little activity with the decline of moonshining. The answer (at least on paper) was rather simple. Close the small unproductive PODs in the southeast and transfer the assigned agents to the CUE cities where the need existed. And that is exactly what they did.

In North Carolina, it was determined that the PODs to be closed were: Williamston, New Bern, Elizabeth City, Rocky

Mount, Goldsboro, Dunn, Hickory, Salisbury, and Wilkesboro. (Bryson City and Greensboro had been closed previously.) Under the plan, older agents within a year or so of retirement would be re-assigned to the closet POD not affected. A few of the agents would also be re-assigned to PODs within the District that needed additional staffing. But the majority would be transferred, and in the Charlotte District that would be Chicago. Well, you can imagine the effect that the announcement had on the agents in those PODs. People started calling their congressmen, senators, judges, local politicians, ministers, and anyone else they thought might be of help. Some were successful, but most were not. Only Elizabeth City and Wilkesboro were granted reprieves, and they, too, were later closed when the politics "got right".

I suppose the closures and re-assignments in theory seemed a perfect solution to the two problems. However, in practice it was a disaster. Here you have these agents in the south who had never worked anything but liquor in the rural woods and fields, and they are abruptly being sent hundreds of miles away to work firearms and explosives cases in the streets of Chicago. To say the least, it was not an ideal situation and certainly not conducive to a successful and productive result.

The CUE coordinators spoke of the challenges in obtaining office space, radios, vehicles, and other related equipment needed to facilitate the rapid shift of personnel. And the effect on the human side was addressed by one of the CUE SACs who reported that… "personnel problems are very, very heavy. Many of the transferred agents have had difficulty in selling their homes. Until those are sold and the families move to the area, the agent's hearts and souls are someplace else. The cost of homes is also a problem in this area for transfers from areas of the country where housing costs are lower."

Of the fifty-five experienced agents transferred to Chicago, forty-six were from the Southeast Region. I am told most of the agents were cooperative and enthusiastic, and really tried to adapt to the change and some were successful to varying degrees. Some were not.

The whole Project CUE fiasco, like most government solutions to address real or perceived problems, started out with good intentions but turned out with a bad ending. ATF lost a number of good, young agents who simply chose not to go and subject themselves and their families to the chaos. Some were able to transfer to other agencies, and some just resigned. Bruce Bassett of the Salisbury POD transferred to another agency and Steve Barrow of Elizabeth City resigned. In the end, most if not all, the agents who went to Chicago and other CUE cities were able over time to find a way back home to the southeast.

While the Reorganization and Project CUE were utmost in the minds of those in the Southeast Region, other things were happening as well. Nationally, John Krogman was appointed Deputy Director and John Corbin retired as Assistant Director (Criminal Enforcement). Locally, agents were still spending most of their time on liquor enforcement activities, although the emphasis from above was changing to firearms and explosives. I think even the hardcore liquor agents knew that the good ole days of moonshining were coming to a close. If there were any doubts, the closure of the small PODs and shifting the agents to the large cities made it semi-official.

The Raleigh POD area of responsibility increased dramatically with the closure of the Rocky Mount, Dunn, New Bern, and Elizabeth City offices. Its territory went from eight counties to more than thirty. Stills and moonshine seizures were still being made in Franklin, Johnston, Durham, and Granville counties, but they were becoming few and far between.

Perry Anderson

Special Agent Perry Anderson of the Nashville office won the "Name the Newsletter" contest to name the Southeast Region newsletter. The winning title was *The Southeasterner*. Perry was a North Carolinian and, like me, a graduate of Pembroke State University. Prior to coming on with ATF in 1975, Perry worked at Halifax Community College and served as a training officer for the North Carolina ABC Board. After applying with ATF, Perry regularly came by the Raleigh office to talk with RAC Herb Steely and me checking on any ATF hiring news. Perry was the distinguished graduate in his CIS and NAT classes and later received a Treasury Department Award for distinguished, exceptional, or meritorious service.

J. W. Perry's Store

J.W. Perry's Store was located in the Pearces section of Franklin County. Despite its rural location, the store was one of the largest gun stores in North Carolina. People came from all over the state to Perry's Store to buy, sell, and trade guns. Every Fourth of July he would have an open house with barbeque and various types of entertainment — sharp shooters, fast draw exhibitors, etc.

Gun dealers in surrounding counties, especially Durham, were constantly calling the Raleigh office to complain about Perry's business practices and how they were losing customers and sales as a result. In Durham and some of the other counties there was a waiting period for obtaining a pistol permit and purchasing a firearm. Franklin County had no such waiting period. Back then the state pistol permit law was interpreted to mean that you could obtain a permit in your county of residence as well as the county in which the purchase was being made. So, a residence of Durham County could go to Franklin County and obtain a permit from the Sheriff's Department (J.W. was an auxiliary deputy) and make his purchase the same trip.

As the complaints intensified, Mike assigned me to do an audit of Perry's gun sales records for the most recent a six-month period. He wanted to determine how many Durham County residents were purchasing guns there and to look at multiple sales to individuals. I completed the examination of the records and reported to Mike that there were an inordinate number of sales to Durham County residents, and that I had found a few individuals with multiple transactions. I informed him that one individual had over two dozens transactions during the period. He asked me who and I told him Mike Zetts. Mike was an avid hunter and gun enthusiast. It was not uncommon for him to buy a particular gun for a specific hunting outing and then trade it back to J.W. when the hunt was over. There, of course, was nothing wrong or illegal, Mike just liked buying and trading guns, as do a lot of people who hunt and are gun enthusiasts.

J.W. was very knowledgeable about firearms and their value, and was also a shrewd businessman who came out on top in most transactions. But there was one time when things did not work out for him. J.W. reported to Mike that someone had stolen a couple of his rifles and Mike asked me to look into it. After listening to his story, it became apparent that J.W. had been set up and came out on the wrong end of the stick (probably one of the few times).

A Sam H had stopped by the store on two or three occasions looking at various long guns. He seemed really interested in two Weatherby rifles, and told J.W. he was going to buy them soon. He returned on a Friday late in the afternoon and again expressed an interest in the two rifles, and finally said he would take them.

As he wrote out the check, he commented it was after 5:00 pm and the banks were closed, and he was sure he (JW) would want to verify the checks; so he would just wait to a later time to buy them (greed is entering the picture here). J.W. said, "No, that's okay, I feel like I know you and I am a pretty good judge of character." So he paid and left with the rifles. And of course, the check was still bouncing when J.W. tried to cash it on Monday.

It turns out Sam H was a professional con man with prior convictions for obtaining property by false pretense and theft. I wrote the case, charging him violations of the GCA of 1968. He was indicted and an arrest warrant was issued, but no Sam H could be found. We learned that he was driving a red Cherokee and using a credit card in a fictitious name and were able to keep up with his movements in and out of the state.

We learned that he had purchased the Jeep in a similar manner as the rifles. In that instance, he went to a local dealer, picked out the Jeep, completed an application, and gave them a bad check for a down payment. During the application he was told that they would have to call his employer to verify his employment. He told them that was fine, but they should wait until after lunch as it was a small office and everyone took lunch at the same time. So they waited and later called the phone number he gave them and was told that he was, in fact, an employee and verified his income.

Yes, you guessed it, they were talking to Sam H. He hurried back, gave them the check, signed the papers, and was off in his new Jeep. He was finally caught by a North Carolina Highway Patrol trooper, who spotted the car in Smithfield and found he was wanted by ATF. I went to Smithfield and arrested him. The ride back was very entertaining, as he was quite a character and seemed to enjoy telling about his cons and swindles.

The Old Timers

The transition period was a very difficult and frustrating time for some of the older agents, many of whom had come to ATF from state and local liquor enforcement agencies and had never worked anything but liquor enforcement. They did not want to make the transition to firearms and explosives investigations, and probably could not have made the transition anyway. They would simply mark time until their retirement time came. A number of them became very resentful with hard feelings and extreme bitterness toward the agency and some individuals in particular.

Mike Zetts at the Raleigh POD was one of those individuals. Mike was the IC (Investigator in Charge) and my first supervisor. Back then, the supervisor position was not a desk job, as it would later become. He worked investigations just like all the other investigators.

In 1972, the Area Supervisor position was eliminated and Area Supervisor Herb Steely stepped back to the RAC (IC became RAC), leaving Mike out in the cold as just a field agent. Other than his pride being hurt a little, the change really did not affect him much. He was getting the same pay and he was still working liquor.

Then in 1975 he was again designated the RAC when Herb Steely was promoted and transferred to Washington. Things did not go well for Mike from the outset, and he was continuously in conflict with SAC Westra and ASAC Whitlow. Simply put, Mike did not like and could not get along with either of them, and I think the feelings were mutual. He would not follow directives and policies, didn't return their calls, and, in effect, just tried to ignore them. It all finally came to a head when Mike became eligible for retirement. He and D.C. Lawson both retired, and I know in Mike's case, with a deep-seated bitterness toward the agency and some of his former co-workers.

Years after I retired, Mike's wife Anita came to me and asked if I would talk to her about Mike being so bitter toward ATF. She said that up to the day of his death, he thought he had been treated unfairly, forced to retire, and held a grudge against ATF and some people in the agency. She said he pretty much kept the details to himself, and she really needed to know what happened to make him feel so bitter.

I told her that he, and others, were victims of the changing times. ATF was changing from liquor enforcement into other areas totally unfamiliar and foreign to the things they had been trained for and done throughout their careers. Mike did not want to change and probably could not have adapted to the changes taking place. Those above him had accepted (some reluctantly) the changing landscape and were pushing for its implementation, and Mike **did not** like to be pushed.

Mike was a good man and a good investigator, and well thought of by his peers. He was always helpful, encouraging and supportive to me from the outset, and I respected and admired him. He was a very positive influence and mentor to me in my early career.

My Last Moonshine

Like the beginning of my moonshine encounters, the end also occurred in a flurry of activity. Over the summer of 1976, I was involved in three moonshine liquor seizures and two distillery seizures. And then there was no more moonshine (for me).

In June, we found a copper pot still in Johnston County. Along with Johnston County ABC officers Guy Lee and James Barefoot, we watched the still periodically over a few days and later seized and destroyed it. It consisted of a 180-gallon copper still, 1,050 gallons of mash and forty-two gallons of liquor. We knew the still actually belonged to a Wake County bootlegger, but he never came to the still.

Also in June, working with the Chatham County Sheriff's Department, we seized ten gallons of moonshine in Siler City. That small seizure led to the seizure of 120 gallons of moonshine and a car in Greensboro and the arrest of the driver who was en route to Chatham County. In early August, we seized 192 gallons of liquor and a truck in Chatham County, and arrested two men.

In August, Special Agent Calcote and I traveled to Elizabeth City to assist Special Agent Garrison in a liquor investigation. We found and seized a distillery in Perquimans County, and arrested two moonshiners. It was my last still raid and, strangely enough, "the only one" I have no recollection of at all.

Two new agents reported to the Raleigh POD during the year: David McAleer came on from a police department in Mississippi, and David Lazar came on from the Dekalb County Police Department in Atlanta.

Special Agent of the Year

Based primarily on the wagering and Perry cases, Mike nominated me for the Southeast Region Special Agent of the Year Award given annually to the "outstanding Special Agent" in the region. I am not sure when the Award was started, but it apparently ended in 1976, the year that for all practical purposes the Southeast Region itself ended.

Bob Powell of the Wilkesboro office received the award in 1973; Mike Hopkins of the Greenville, Tennessee office won in 1974; Jim Roberts of the Meridian, Mississippi office won in 1975; and Andy Pate of the Greenville, South Carolina office stole the award from me in 1976 (just kidding, Andy). In 1977, George Bradley of the Chattanooga, Tennessee office received the National Special Agent of the Year award.

Chapter Eleven
MOONSHINE TO MANAGEMENT (1977-1978)

Nationally, the Carter administration announced plans for a major reorganization of federal law enforcement. The plan would move ATF explosives and firearms functions into the Justice Department. Tobacco and alcohol functions would remain in the Treasury Department. The plan also included a shift of the Border Patrol from the Justice Department's Immigration and Naturalization Service to form a new border management agency in the Treasury Department. The implementation of the plan was delayed and eventually dropped as far as the ATF changes.

The Southeast Region and moonshine liquor era pretty much came to an end in 1977 with the retirement of Bill Griffin. Mr. Griffin came on with ATF in 1948 in Kentucky, and moved up the ranks to become the Assistant Regional Commissioner of ATF for the Internal Revenue Service in 1967. He served as the ARC and later as the Regional Director when ATF came out from under the IRS.

In March, I attended the ATF Basic Supervisory School in Alexandria, Virginia. As the name would indicate, the class was for first line supervisors with the basics of the job and responsibilities. I enjoyed the school and recall it was very informative. However, the one thing that sticks out had nothing to do with the school but was about sports. The UNC Tarheels were playing Marquette in the NCAA basketball finals. While I was a Duke fan and didn't care too much for the Heels, it looked like perhaps a good opportunity to pick up a little cash when talk of betting on the game came up. After all, this was a very good team led by All American Phil Ford, and I could not believe they could be beaten by Marquette. How could I have known that Ford had injured his hand and would only score six points?

The loss cost me a few hundred dollars — them "damn Heels". Marquette was considered by some to be only the fourth best team in the finals, and to this day some of the hardcore Heels think that there was a conspiracy to fix the game to give Al McGuire a championship before he retired. Who knows?

While we were still working liquor at the Raleigh POD as well as elsewhere in the district, the shift to firearms investigation was picking up steam. In April, an undercover investigation was conducted in Henderson of an unlicensed firearms dealer. The case resulted in the purchase/seizure of two pen guns, a mortar, and twenty-three other firearms, and the arrest of the unlicensed dealer.

Acting Resident Agent in Charge (RAC)

Although working cases and assisting others, my primary responsibility was as supervisor of the Raleigh POD. I had been acting RAC since the prior November, when Mike retired. Throughout the period SAC Westra had said that I would become the RAC as soon as things could be worked out. Of course, I didn't know then and still am not sure exactly why it takes so long to "work things out".

It seems that the plan was that Bobby Marshall was being transferred out of the District Office to Headquarters, Group Supervisor Stan Noel would move over to the District Office to replace Bobby, and I would replace Stan as Group Supervisor. From that point on through the time I retired, it seemed like it took forever to get through the bureaucratic layers to simply make a promotion or fill a vacancy, sometimes several months as it turned out in this case.

I suspect that if Mr. Griffin had still been in charge that would not have been the case. As noted in chapter 1, under his command such decisions and actions were usually done pretty quickly. In fact, I recall in 1972 or '73, Herb Steely called me into his office on a Monday morning and said, "I probably should not even tell you this, but I got a call last Friday informing me that you were being transferred to Wilmington." He added that rather than tell me then and possibly ruin my weekend, he had decided to wait until Monday morning. He then said, "…but I got a call this morning and was told you would not be transferred to Wilmington after all." Go figure.

In May or June, Mr. Westra called and said he had gotten the go ahead to fill the RAC positions at Raleigh and Charlotte. He went on to say that I had first choice, and Ken Brady would get the other. I asked him if I could think about it a few days and he said yes. Being young and somewhat idealist, I decided it would be difficult for me (and for them) to supervise the agents I had worked with and came to know over the years, so I decided on Charlotte. The fact that I had my house for sale and if I transferred to Charlotte the government would pay the expenses for the sale had nothing to do with my decision (I hope). I informed Mr. Westra, and he agreed it was probably the right choice.

So on August 16th, the teletype came out announcing Ken's promotion to RAC in Raleigh, and my promotion to RAC/Group Supervisor in Charlotte. Coincidently, it was the day that Elvis died.

Moonshine To Management — Take One

On September 12th I reported to the Charlotte office located in an office building on Park Road, south of town. (The office had moved there from the downtown location on Morehead Street, where I was sworn in). After the obligatory orientation in the district Office, I walked down the hall to the POD office and started what would turn out to be a rather short adventure. Connie Stroud was the POD clerk, and Special Agents were Jerry Pistole, Bill Vassar, Henry Byrd, Dick Wiggins, Roger Brown, and Richard Fox.

Pistole, Vassar, and Brown had been Charlotte for some time, and Byrd I believe had been a Regional Special until that position was eliminated. Wiggins had transferred in from Tennessee, and Fox from the Wilkesboro POD during the CUE moves. Bob Martin, the long-time RAC in Salisbury, was assigned to the Charlotte office on paper after his POD was closed under CUE, but was just marking time to his retirement. Dale Winters, a new agent came, on a few months later.

During the first few months things were going well and I was enjoying the new job and location. I stayed in Mr. Westra's cabin on Lake Willey for several weeks until my house sold in Raleigh and my family moved to Charlotte. We initially bought a house in Old Providence, a nice subdivision south of Charlotte, but later sold it and bought a bigger house in Mint Hill. But it wasn't too long before the newness started to wear off and the realities of the new job and situation became apparent, and the seeds of dissatisfaction and discontentment started to grow. It was not any one single thing, but a series of events and circumstances led me to start to question my supervisory abilities.

First of all, being next to the District Office has its benefits, but also sometimes can create problems for POD supervisor. The benefit was that the SAC and ASAC were just next door and I could have quick access when needed. However, on the downside, the SAC and ASAC were just next door and could, and often did, drop in for a visit just to talk and see how things are going.

As Ed Garrison once said when he was a one-man POD in Elizabeth City, you don't have to worry about the SAC or ASAC just dropping in unannounced (it is six hours from Charlotte to Elizabeth City). Coupled with the fact they were just next door, their idea of the RACs job had changed from part-time supervisor who still did investigations, to that of full-time supervisor who was expected to be in the office a majority of time.

While neither Mr. Westra nor Mr. Whitlow were overly dictatorial or hands-on, you were expected to know and follow their policies and their way of doing things, whether you agreed or not. There were a few times when they got involved in what I considered minor personnel issues and tried to make them much bigger deals than they actually were.

A few months into the job, a case report submitted by agent Bill Vassar came back from the District Office for some changes and corrections. The process was the agent would prepare his case report, send it to the RAC for review and changes if needed, and then he would forward to the District for final review and approval before going to the US Attorney for prosecution. Depending on the reviewer and his idea of what should and should not be in the report (they both changed often), case reports were often returned to make changes to more reflect the reviewer and District's thinking.

Bill Vassar, having gone to law school, was one who used a lot of words to say something that perhaps could have been said with fewer just as well. For example, when describing his seizure of still in Iredell County, he might start out something like it was a beautiful day when I left the office and my drive to Iredell County was so refreshing with the onset of autumn in the air, the changing colors of the flowers and leaves from green to assorted colors of red, gold, yellow, brown, etc. Well, at this particular time the "Joe Friday, Just the Facts" style was in vogue as far as case reports. They did not want any flowery words but just the bare facts of what you did.

So back to the Vassar case report that was returned for corrections and changes, primarily to just get rid of a lot of what the reviewer considered excessive and unnecessary verbiage. I handed the report to Bill and told him the changes they wanted made. He just stared at me for a while and then threw the report to the floor and said, "If they want the damn report changed tell them they can do it, I am not." For what seemed an eternity (although in reality just a few seconds), I was standing there thinking, "What do I do now?"

In my mind, I was frantically running through the pages of the Supervisors Manual to find that section that addressed how to handle this situation. Not finding anything, I reached down, picked up the report and carried it over to the District Office and relayed to them Bill's suggestion as to how the corrections might best be accomplished. They apparently agreed, for the case report was not returned and I never heard anything else about it.

All things were not that bad; I had some good experiences while there. I attended the Union Grove Fiddler Convention as part of a law enforcement contingency of state and local officers to monitor some activities there. I presume it had to do with suspected illegal activity related to liquor, guns, or drugs. I had an occasion to re-meet SA Joe Kopka, who had become an Inspector in HQ Internal Affairs after leaving Raleigh, and to assist him in an investigation involving a District agent. One of our agents had been arrested for being intoxicated and possessing marijuana. As it turned out, the alleged marijuana was a bag of cut greens and other vegetables to be used in the making of turtle soup. It was determined the agent was a victim of poor judgment (his own) in the friends he was associating with, and an unbelievable (and sometimes comical) series of events leading to the charges which were ultimately dismissed.

The highlight of my time in Charlotte was a trip to Boston. One of the agents, Richard Fox I think, had an investigation on a local man who was supposedly converting AR-15's to fully automatic and selling them. It was determined that one of his buyers was in Boston, and he was going to travel to Boston by bus and make the delivery. By a stroke of luck, I got the assignment to observe the suspect get on the bus in Charlotte and then fly to Boston to observe him getting off the bus. Once there, I assisted Boston Special Agent Timothy Reedy in the arrest and seizure of the AR-15's. Also while there, I got a tour of the city and best of all, got to experience a Red Sox game in Fenway Park.

In May, we moved the District Office and POD from Park Road to Church Street in downtown Charlotte. The move, we were told, was a result of President Carter's directive that government agencies should relocate to the inner cities to help with the revitalization of the cities. The preparation and actual move consumed a lot of my time and attention. Mr. Westra and I spent a lot of time designing and actually building the evidence/firearms vault in the basement garage of the new building.

In June and July, my discontent and dissatisfaction with the job really started to wear on me mentally and physically to the point I knew I had to do something. I often had headaches, chest pain, and discomfort to the point I thought I was having a heart attack. I finally and reluctantly informed Mr. Westra of the situation, and requested to step down from the job and return to Raleigh as a field agent.

He seemed surprised and I expect to some extent disappointed, and maybe even betrayed having given me the promotion. He tried to talk me out of it and encouraged me to just hang on another year and you will be going to HQ. I told him that I did not want to go to HQ, and in fact the inevitable move there in a year or so was one of the reasons I wanted to return to the field. (The "Whack a RAC" program had just been initiated, wherein RAC's after two years of supervisory experience could expect, like it or not, a transfer to HQ for the betterment of the Bureau. Some of the whacked RACs including Bill Benson, I think, had stopped by the Charlotte Office on their forced journey up I-85 to DC.)

After agreeing to pay all relocation expenses myself with no cost to the government, Mr. Westra told me to put the request in writing and he would approve it. I did and he did. While I didn't question his reasoning, it did open up a slot for Bobby Marshall to return from HQ. And he mentioned there was a new cigarette smuggling law coming and that he might want me to get involved with it in

Raleigh. Of interest, the move to Charlotte, including the sale of my residence in Raleigh and purchase in Charlotte and all related relocation expenses, cost the government about $20,000. My return trip to Raleigh cost me about $500, with the main expense being the rental of a U-Haul truck. I sold my house in Mint Hill to Agent John Lorrick, who had just returned from Chicago, thereby avoiding paying costly real estate fees.

In August, I was back in Raleigh as a field agent eager to get back to work. My headaches, anxieties, and chest pains (real or imagined) were gone and the job was about to be fun again. Congress was about to pass a new federal law on cigarette smuggling, and North Carolina was considered the primary source state for cigarettes. We envisioned it would be moonshine enforcement reborn with cigarettes being the commodity rather than liquor. We would again be locating stashes, cultivating and working informants, conducting surveillances, conducting raids, and making arrests. The old liquor guys (those few remaining) were getting excited again, something they just couldn't get into with the firearms investigations.

Part Two

GUNS, BOMBS & BUTTS
(1979 – 1994)

Chapter Twelve
CIGARETTE SMUGGLING

T he federal Trafficking in Contraband Cigarettes law was passed and signed by the President in November 1978, and ATF was given the responsibility for enforcing the new law. The purpose of the bill, according to ATF HQ, was "to provide for a federal role in the fight against cigarette smuggling and to provide a timely solution to a serious organized crime problem."

HQ went on to say, "Our primary goal is to investigate large scale violations which are complex in nature and involve organized suppliers and distributors of contraband cigarettes in substantial quantities. All investigations concerning alleged violations of the law will be closely monitored at Bureau HQ and only those which meet this criteria will be authorized."

Training classes were scheduled and SACs were instructed to start gathering intelligence on cigarette smuggling within their respective districts. At the outset, we were to assess the problem and to gather intelligence on current smuggling activities.

Cigarette smuggling or butt-legging (I like that better) came about in the 1960s as a result of the disparity in state tax rates on cigarettes. For example, the state tax rate on a pack of cigarettes in North Carolina was 2 cents, while in New York City it was 23 cents (state and local). A carton of cigarettes (ten packs) in North Carolina would have a 20- cent tax cost while in New York the tax cost would be $2.30, translating to a price difference of $2.10 per carton. So on 1,000 cartons for example, an enterprising fellow (or organization) in New York could make a profit of $2,100 quite easily on a day trip to North Carolina and back. An added incentive was that there was very little chance of getting caught. In North Carolina, you could buy as many cartons as you wanted and not violate any law, and in New York City you would only be violating tax laws and regulations, which I am sure carried minor penalties. With estimated tax losses to the so-called high-tax state ranging up to $400 million annually, they began pushing for the federal government to step in by passing a law making the bootlegging of cigarettes illegal.

The states themselves had put forth an effort to curtail the smuggling within their states, but with limited success due primarily to the fact of the multi-State nature of the problem. To address the multi-jurisdiction issues, several states joined together to create formal organizations to combat smuggling. Probably the most successful of the joint ventures was the Eastern Seaboard Cigarette Tax Enforcement Group (ESICTEG), which consisted of nine members — Connecticut, Delaware, Maryland, Massachusetts, New Jersey, New York State, New York City, Pennsylvania, and the Northern Virginia Tax Commissions. ESICTEG officers worked primarily within their member states, but on occasions ventured into North Carolina to conduct covert surveillance operations. Roanoke Rapids and Weldon were favorite target areas for the covert surveillances because within both towns, there were known cigarette suppliers. And perhaps another reason might have been that the towns were located on I-95 just inside North Carolina border, and if things went bad, they could easily high-tail it back across the Virginia line to safety. And when on occasion their presence was discovered by local authorities, they "were asked to leave and don't come back ya'll". Although sometimes threatened with jail, I am told none of the "Yankee spies" were ever actually jailed.

Unable to substantially impact the smuggling and high revenue losses themselves, the high-loss tax states turned to politics and the federal government for help. They focused their efforts on Congress, and as a result the Trafficking in Contraband Cigarette law was passed. The federal law (unlike most federal laws) was relatively limited and simple. The law prohibited the transportation, receipt, shipment, possession, distribution or purchase of more than 60,000 cigarettes (300 cartons) bearing tax indicia of a state other than the State in which they were found. For example, if an individual possessed more than 300 cartons of cigarettes in New York with a North Carolina tax stamp he would be in violation of the federal statute.

Violation of the statute was punishable by imprisonment up to five years and/or a fine of up to $100,000. Vehicles used to transport contraband cigarettes were subject to seizure. The law also required the seller of more than 60,000 cigarettes to maintain dis-position records to show the name, address, destination, vehicle licenses number, driver's license number, and signature of the pur-chaser. Violations of the record keeping requirement was punish-able by imprisonment up to three years and/or a fine up to $5,000. Interestingly, the law did not require a specific bound record or did not allow for open inspection of records. Theoretically, a person could jot down the required information on the back of a match pad and throw it in a drawer and be in compliance. As to inspec-tion, records could only be inspected by consent or judicial order.

Back in the Charlotte District we were gearing up to take on the cigarette smugglers. SAC Westra assigned me to be the Tobacco Enforcement Coordinator and designated sixteen other Special Agents to cigarette enforcement. It was recognized that to have any success it would be necessary to become familiar with the distribu-tion system from the manufacturer to the end consumer, to obtain the cooperation and records from the NC Department of Revenue, and to engage and obtain information from enforcement agencies within the high-tax-loss states as to their cooperation and intelli-gence on smuggling activities.

SAC Westra and I met with representatives of all the manufac-tures in North Carolina, all of whom seemed agreeable and forth-coming to cooperate. Of particular assistance was Jack Medlin of Liggett and Meyers Tobacco in Durham. Jack was very informative and cooperative from the outset, and later served as a guest instruc-tor at some of our training classes. We learned that cigarettes go from the manufacturer to licensed stamping agents within the vari-ous states, then to the retailer for sale to the user.

In states other than North Carolina, cigarettes were shipped from the manufacturer to public warehouses and then picked up by the stamping agents (presumably because most manufacturers were located in NC and direct shipment to the stamping agents is more feasible). The stamping agents purchase and apply the tax stamps. In North Carolina, the stamping agents purchases the stamps and accounts for the 2-cent per pack to the NC Depart-ment of Revenue, they then applied the stamps (either decal or Pit-ney Bowes inked impression) to the individual packs of cigarettes and distributed them to the various retailers. Manufacturers also distributed cigarettes to military exchanges and Indian reservations where no state tax was paid. Although early on the possibility of Indian reservation cigarettes being a problem, we were told "don't mess with the Indians" and we didn't.

It was also recognized at the outset that cooperation from the state of North Carolina would be essential. After all, they knew who the licensed stamping agents were and their location, as well as information on quantities purchased and taxes paid. It was a well-established fact that most of the cigarettes seized in the high-tax states had come from North Carolina. Some officials in those states felt that NC was not doing anything to help and were, in fact, complicit in the smuggling.

In response to these accusations and growing negative press both outside and within the state, Governor Jim Hunt publicly said that cigarette smuggling is a crime with serious implications for the State, and his administration was strongly committed to aid the anti-smuggling efforts. In a letter to me, the Governor restated his commitment, and called for a task force group to meet to discuss recommendations as to how North Carolina could be of assistance in the federal effort.

The meeting was held in which Gary Pearce, the Governor's Press Secretary, reiterated the Governor's commitment to do everything possible to aid in the anti-smuggling effort. I think his commitment was reinforced by the fact that the heads of the Department of Revenue, State Bureau of Investigation, State Highway Patrol, and the Deputy Attorney General along with their respective staffs were in attendance. Each offered their full support and inquired as to what their respective departments could do.

I, representing ATF, outlined the new federal law and ATF's role in enforcing the law, and explained that cooperation was welcomed from all but the most needed information at this time was Department of Revenue records pertaining to licensed stampers/wholesalers. Secretary of Revenue Mark Lynch stated that all requested information was available and would immediately be supplied to ATF.

However, (now enter the lawyers) one of the Attorney General's staff raised the question of whether or not the records could be released under the recently enacted NC Privacy Act. It seems that the act prohibited the Revenue Department from releasing any tax records or information to anyone other than the IRS or specific law enforcement agencies of the state of North Carolina. He explained that the act had been as a result of pressure from the IRS, who insisted that if the policy of exchanging tax information between the state and IRS was to continue, the State Privacy Act was necessary to insure the integrity of the IRS information. (Here again we have one federal agency preventing another from doing their job.) After a lengthy discussion as to possible ways to get around the privacy issue, several suggestions were made ranging from amending the State law to requesting that the IRS release the information directly to ATF. It was decided that neither was feasible, and the best approach was to make no high-level formal recommendation, but "just let the working-level individuals work it out", and we did.

Subsequent to the meeting, I met with Alcohol Law Enforcement (ALE) Supervisor Al Felton, who had been designated by the Governor to investigate and monitor the cigarette smuggling situation as it related to possible violations of North Carolina laws. I had worked with Al back in the "liquor days", and he was very cooperative and helpful as we tried to get a handle on what was going on in NC. Special Agent Bob Barber of the SBI was assigned to the investigation, and he and I worked together on daily basis checking out information and running down leads. We met weekly with Secretary of the Revenue Lynch whose department cooperated fully with the effort.

In March, the Charlotte District hosted a conference in Durham to discuss the new law and ATF's enforcement strategies. Personnel from various state and local enforcement agencies as well as ATF agents assigned to work cigarette smuggling attended the conference. Intelligence on smuggling activities were exchanged and contacts were made with the various agencies. After obtaining a list of stamping agents and additional intelligence, statewide surveillances were conducted of various suspected outlets throughout the state. ATF agents from New York, Massachusetts, and Pennsylvania, as well as state and local officers from high-tax loss areas, were brought in to assist in the surveillance.

While intelligence indicated some suspect outlets in the Winston-Salem and Raleigh, the majority of the suspected sources were along the I-95 corridor from Weldon to Fayetteville. While some activity was observed during the various surveillances, they failed to disclose evidence of massive smuggling operations. The effort was hampered to some extent by cultural and language differences and to a lesser extent the weather. For example, we had an agent call in on the radio to the Raleigh office asking for directions to the office. When asked his location, he said he was in Algiers to which we replied it was going to be very difficult to get from Algiers to the Raleigh office by car. As it turns out he was actually in Angier, a small town about twenty miles from Raleigh.

As to the weather, during one of the surveillances we were hit with a two-day snow storm. Imagine spending three days snowed-in at the Holiday Inn in Roanoke Rapids with Bob Creighton, Will Blocker, Joe Wilson and others. We played a lot of cards and fortunately for some (and unfortunately for others) there was a liquor store in the parking lot of the motel.

The disappointing results of the surveillance projects not withstanding, we continued our enforcement effort in the District. In fact, we hosted an ESICTEG meeting in Atlantic Beach in 1983. As we continued and intensified our enforcement effort, it started to become apparent that the extent of the smuggling was not what it was thought to be. Not only were we in the Charlotte District not finding much, the ESICTEC agents were reporting very little activity within their respective states. They reported they were getting very little information and were not making any seizures.

There were some successes, most of which were early on. In March 1979, Special Agent Garrison of the Elizabeth City office developed information on a cigarette supplier in his area selling cigarettes to New York smugglers. He learned that a large load of cigarettes would be leaving headed north. With the assistance of Marshall Reece in the ATF plane, we followed the large truck to a remote campground in Winchester, Virginia, where cigarettes were off loaded into a van and truck bearing New York plates. Both vehicles departed separately heading north.

We broke the surveillance teams in half and continued the surveillance of the two vehicles. Garrison and I, along with agents McAleer and Lazar, followed the van while others tailed the truck. As we continued north through Pennsylvania, local agents there were alerted and joined in the surveillance. As we approached

New York City, the ATF plane had to drop off as it was entering restricted airspace. Unknown to us at the time, the driver of the van had spotted our surveillance back in Pennsylvania and his plan was to take us into the city and lose us. Well, it almost worked, as he lost everyone but Ed and me. He started running lights, getting off and on the highway, slowing and speeding up to the point it became obvious he had made us.

Now you have got to get the picture here. We had been following this vehicle all night and we hit New York City in the morning at rush hour. The driver of the van (who knows the city) is aware of the tail and is going to shake us in the city. Ed and I know that we are the only surveillance car still on the van, and he will probably eventually lose us, too.

We have no idea where we are at and no way of getting assistance. So, we decided to take him down even though we had been told several times "we are only to gather intelligence on the smuggling activity and to make no arrest". Well, we put the blue light (we later learned the red light was law enforcement there) and siren on him and he pulled over at "10th and Prospect" in Brooklyn. We got the driver, Walter H. out of the van and observed several hundred cartons of cigarettes in the van.

As we pondered, "Now we got him what are we going to do with him", a New York ATF agent came driving up. He got out and asked us what was going on and we advised him of the situation. He reinforced the message that we (ATF) were not to make any arrests. So, Ed and I un-arrested him and turned him and the cigarettes over to New York state and city authorities, who arrested him and seized the cigarettes and van.

We later all managed to find the ATF office and gathered there to give our report to the ATF SAC and the local authorities. Already an air of reservation and perhaps a little mistrust, it did not help things when Agent McAleer, tired and sleepy, referred to New York SAC Mike LaPerch as Mr. LaTrout. But we all overcame and got along just fine. We learned that the other truck had been followed to a warehouse in the city and more than 5,500 cartons were seized and three people had been arrested on state charges.

As we continued to discuss the seizure, Agent McAleer looked out the window down to the street and saw that his government car was gone and surmised it had been stolen or towed. A New York agent said you better hope it was stolen, because your chance of getting it back will be better than if it had been towed. They made some calls to try to find it, which was complicated by the fact we didn't know the license number. We always kept some untraceable license plates in the trunk, and the only thing we could say for sure that it was a New Jersey plate. Somehow the car was located in an impound lot where it had been towed for improper parking. With a little help from an impound officer, we "reclaimed" the car from the impound lot and headed back south down I-95.

Sometime later, Ed and I were subpoenaed by New York authorities to testify in the case. After determining there were no outstanding warrants for us (theft of a motor vehicle), we returned to New York for the trial. We sat in court all day, but the case was never called and was continued over to the next day. I must say court and related practices and procedures are a little different up there. Ed stayed over to the next day and testified in the case and I went home.

Also in March, special agents in Raleigh developed information that a local resident was involved in smuggling large quantities of cigarettes to a northern state. Subsequent investigation resulted in the seizure of 3,187 cartons of cigarettes in Rhode Island and the arrest of two. Later on, Fayetteville agents developed information on a smuggling operation from Sanford, North Carolina to Michigan. As a result of surveillance on the supplier, a large U-Haul truck was observed being loaded with numerous cases of cigarettes. A mobile surveillance was conducted to attempt to follow the cigarettes to Michigan to identify and catch the whole smuggling ring. However, we ran into a blinding snowstorm just south of Charleston, West Virginia, and went ahead and stopped the truck. We seized 3,194 cartons of cigarettes and arrested two individuals in the truck. The Charleston agents assisted in the arrests and seizure. It was good to see SA John Spidell (former Raleigh agent), who was the supervisor of the Charleston office.

In addition to the over the road smuggling, information was developed that there were mail order operations going on within the state. Special Agents Lazar and McAleer uncovered a major cigarette mail order business operating in Farmville, North Carolina.

Over a period of several months, their investigation and surveillance in Farmville revealed that Norris E. and Ray P. were partners in large-scale mail-order business shipping out approximately 6,000 cartons a week. Their investigation resulted in search warrants being executed in North Carolina as well as in Texas, Florida, Massachusetts, and elsewhere, resulting in the seizure of cigarettes shipped by the partners. The investigation resulted in the indictment and arrest of Norris E. and Ray P. and eight others in the Federal Eastern Judicial District of NC Court. Norris E. and Ray P. pled guilty and were sentenced to prison terms. The remaining defendant pled to lesser charges and received probation.

Early on I was detailed to HQ as a temporary operations officer to help in ATF's tobacco program. Being a new program with very little knowledge known of the activity, HQ was looking for someone to plan and run the program. Although I was never asked by anyone in authority, a couple people (Bill Benson and Jerry Robinson as I recall) inquired as to my interest in doing so to which I politely said, "Thanks, but NO thanks". Agent Joe Bredehoft of the New York office (probably the most knowledgeable, best qualified, and most suitable) was asked to take the job and he, too, declined, not wanting to have to transfer to HQTRS. The position, I believe, was eventually given to Andy Vita, who transferred into HQ from Chicago.

As in the case of most situations when things are not going as planned, an attempt was made to find out why not and come up with a solution. To that end, I was asked to do an analysis of the cigarette smuggling problem as it related to North Carolina, with the objective of reaching a determination as to the scope and extent of the problem as it presently existed. It was a pretty tall order, I thought, for a young man with no training and very little knowledge as to how to conduct a scientific study of such a wider-ranging nature. Upon stating my reservations and doubts as to my ability to do the project, I was told, "You know more about it than anyone else, so just do it and we want it done in two weeks."

Primarily based on per capita sales figures for North Carolina for Fiscal Year 1979, it was determined that the number of cartons sold in the state over the national average was 36,473,580 cartons. Surveillances conducted of various retailers along I-95 and I-85 in North Carolina, revealed tremendous sales to tourist and travelers in lots of five to one hundred cartons. This so-called "casual smuggling" was believed to have accounted for most of the excess volume, leaving a small number for over the road smugglers. The report concluded by saying that based on all the factors reviewed, the cigarette smuggling problem in NC had been greatly reduced from what it once was (or once alleged to be) to what actually exists today (1980).

Shortly after completing my report and while still in DC, I got a call from Pat Stith, a reporter for the *Raleigh News and Observer*, asking me how the federal anti-smuggling law was working. Pat had done several pieces on cigarette smuggling, and I had talked with him briefly a few times. We talked for quite a while, and I told him about some of our successes as well as failure to really substantiate that smuggling was actually occurring at the level anticipated. There were no discussions about the conversation being on or off the record, and whether or not he was putting together a major article on cigarette smuggling.

Well, as it turned out, he was doing just that as I found out a few weeks later. I awoke one Sunday morning to a front-page story "Cigarette Smuggling Drops Sharply" in the *Raleigh News and Observer* written by Pat Stith. It was quite extensive and contained a couple of quotes by me—

"We came into this thing in December (enforcing the new federal law) with a lot of publicity. These northern states were crying to Congress that they were losing so much money. We simply have not found that to be true. The cigarette smuggling problem was never as big as officials in their high-tax states said it was. Estimates of tax losses due to cigarette smuggling had been tremendously overstated."

Stith went on to say that he had talked with several officials in the northern states, some of whom conceded that activity was way down and may not have been as extensive as believed in the past.

Upon my return to HQ on Monday morning, I was informed that the Assistant Director-Criminal Enforcement (ADCE) wanted to see me. I reported to his office as instructed and met with Phil McGuire, who I think was the Deputy ADCE at the time. As always, he was very pleasant and amiable and asked me how things were going back in Carolina. Afterwards, however, he pointed out the error of my way in talking with the reporter and speaking for the Bureau. He conceded that I was probably correct in what I had said, but talked about the "big picture" and possible ramifications politically of what I had said. I promised I understood and would not do it again. Although not a term used at that time, my lack of "political correctness" would best summarize the episode.

Having accepted the probability that large quantities of cigarettes were not moving over the road to the high-tax loss states, it was decided that perhaps the problem was an accountability or audit problem within the states themselves.

SA Bredehoft and Inspector Randy Pollard of the Tampa office put together an audit training program that they provided to the various states. Elements of their audit program were also incorporated into a state and local training class that was developed and held several times during the 1980s at the Federal Law Enforcement Training Center (FLETC). In addition to ATF personnel, investigators and auditors from several state and local agencies served as advisers and instructors. Among those participating at various classes were John Mullins, Ron Lewis, Dave Campbell, and Pat Castel of New York; Ron Armstrong of Delaware; Warren Breece and Bill Wigglesworth of Connecticut; Fred Colbert and Steve Aronson of Massachusetts; Ken Ball, Jack Wallace and Claude Cruce from Florida; Larry Strauss from Pennsylvania; and Ron Buchanan of New Jersey.

In spite of the lack of seizures and evidence of large scale smuggling, we continued on in the anti-smuggling effort in North Carolina. We continued checking records, doing surveillances, and other enforcement activity until the point when I was the only ATF agent assigned to tobacco enforcement. SBI agent Bob Barber and I continued working information received and conducting surveillance at suspected cigarette outlets in Raleigh and along the I-95 corridor. In most cases involving small amounts of cigarettes, we furnished the information to officers in the ESICTEG states who made the seizures and arrests. Over time, the above cases notwithstanding, it was becoming increasingly apparent that the level of activity was not what (or what it was alleged to have been) during the 1960s and 70s.

Chapter Thirteen
MOONSHINE OUT – GUNS AND BOMBS IN (1979-1981)

While the new cigarette law was a primary focus in the Charlotte District and to a lesser extent nationally, other things were happening. G.R. Dickerson was named the new ATF Director and Bob Sanders was appointed the ADCE upon the retirement of Miles Keathley. The re-organization and streamlining of Criminal Enforcement was continuing but not as fast as HQ had anticipated, I suspect. In 1979, the Headquarters Office of Criminal Enforcement created four Regional Offices of Investigations to replace the previous regional setup. Those offices in Atlanta, Chicago, New York and San Francisco were to become operational in October 1979.

Dave Edmisten was named the Regional Director of Investigation for the Atlanta office. He started out as a criminal investigator in 1955 and was stationed at offices in North and South Carolina, Georgia and Tennessee. He left the Southeast Region in 1972 to become the Special Agent in Charge of the newly created Cleveland District Office. Dave was a native of Boone, North Carolina and had two other brothers with careers in government service. A younger brother, Baker, was an ATF Special Agent in Dublin, Georgia, but left the agency when that office was closed and agents were transferred during CUE. Another brother, Rufus, was a prominent attorney in the state and came to fame as Chief Counsel to Senator Sam Erwin during the Watergate Hearings in 1974. He later served as Attorney General and Secretary of State in NC and ran unsuccessfully for Governor in 1984.

Liquor is Dead

In the Charlotte District and elsewhere in the southeast, I suspect, there were agents still working liquor daily who could not accept that moonshining was dead and gone. In a memo to all

RACs in February 1979, SAC Westra put it in writing. He wrote that illicit liquor is ATF's last priority, and that some agents were expending excessive time on illicit liquor.

He continued, "there will be no more man-hours expended on illicit liquor unless an agent has <u>very reliable, specific</u> information on the location of a distillery with a utilized mash capacity in excess of <u>1,000 gallons</u>. There will be no time expended on walk-through or fly-through operations of any type, and no more time expended on contacting informers for illicit whiskey information only. Information regarding illicit liquor should be incidental or secondary to the Bureau's priorities of explosives, firearms and cigarettes."

And yet there were still some who would not or could not accept it.

National Response Team (NRT)

In 1979, ATF created the NRT to assist field agents in the investigation of large-scale explosions and fires. The team was made up of experienced agents, Certified Explosives Specialists, Certified Fire Investigators, and laboratory technicians and specialists. The concept was that the NRT would be activated and respond within in 24 hours to major fire and explosives incidents when requested by the field agents. Their primary focus was to determine the cause of the explosion or fire, and if determined to be deliberately set, to identify those responsible. This was usually accomplished by an extensive cause and origin scene investigation and in-depth interviews with owners, employees, and others with information about the incident.

The NRT stayed on scene until the cause and origin was determined, which could be a matter of days to weeks depending on the nature and size of the fire or explosion. The first call out of the team was in May 1979 to Shelby, North Carolina, to investigate a large fire that destroyed a whole block of downtown business buildings. In addition to the estimated five million dollar property loss, four firemen and a gas company employee were killed when a wall collapsed on top of them. The investigation determined that the fire was intentionally set and two men were arrested and charged with murder.

The NRT was very successful and additional teams were established to better respond to the ever-increasing demand for their capabilities and expertise. ATF became recognized as the premier agency in investigating large-scale fires and explosives incidents. Later on, ATF developed the International Response Team (ITR) to respond to fire and explosives scene around the world.

B&B Guns

One of the most significant investigations locally, nationally, and internationally was the B&B Guns case worked by Agent Bob Graham. The investigation was worked in conjunction with US Customs, the US Justice Department, and law enforcement agencies in England and Ireland.

The case originated with the recovery of weapons by Scotland Yard in a London apartment house following a hostage/shootout incident with members of the IRA. One of the weapons seized, a semi-automatic Armalite 180 rifle, was traced to B&B Guns in Wilson, North Carolina.

Working with the various agencies involved, the investigation revealed that two New York men had been purchasing weapons and ammunition for the IRA for a number of years, and that one of their sources for the guns and ammunition was B&B Guns. The investigation revealed that Howard Bruton, Jr., one of the B&B owners, had been supplying guns and ammunition to the two New York men as far back as 1972. The two New York men, George DeMeo and Robert Ferraro, along with Bruton and B&B co-owner Binford Benton were charged with violations of the federal firearms laws. Benton pled guilty to one count and agreed to testify against the others. John Bulla, manager of B&B Guns, also agreed to testify in exchange for immunity from prosecution.

The two-week trial was held in U.S. Eastern District Court in Raleigh with Judge Franklin Dupree presiding. Judge Dupree was a no-nonsense judge who I always found to be rather strict but fair. If he said court was to begin at 9:30, he expected the attorneys and witnesses for both sides to be there at that time. Some, I suspect, would not agree with my characterization as to his fairness. One in particular would be Jeffrey MacDonald, the Army doctor convicted of murdering his wife and two daughters at Ft. Bragg in 1970. He and his team of lawyers were very critical of Judge Dupree and some of his evidentiary rulings made during his trial in 1978.

Benton and Bulla testified that guns and ammunition had been funneled from B& B Guns to DeMeo and Ferraro and then to the IRA as far back as 1972. They testified that the ammunition had been stolen from Camp Lejeune Marine Base. Benton testified he sold 700,000 to one million rounds of stolen ammunition to DeMeo at about a nickel a round, or $50,000. There was testimony that Bruton discussed hiring a hit man to kill Benton and to planting a machine gun in Benton's house to set him up for arrest. Judge Dupree instructed the jury to ignore the statements made by Bulla. Officers from Scotland Yard and Ireland testified in the case relative to the arrest and seizure of the B&B guns in England. After a short deliberation, the jury found all three defendants guilty.

With the hostilities between the British and IRA at that time, security was of a major concern. The Raleigh office was assigned to provide security for the British and Irish officers. We would escort them from the court at the end of the day to their motel, The Royal Villa, and escort them back to court the following morning. On a few occasions, the evenings were spent in the motel lounge having a few beers. Our guests didn't care too much for American beer, characterizing it as being watered down. They, on the other hand, loved their Irish whiskey. They just poured it in a glass and drank it straight with no mixer. They really were a bunch of nice guys and quite entertaining with their stories, specifically involving the ongoing battle with the IRA. A few weeks after the trial, I received a RUC necktie from Ken Masterson, an officer in The Royal Ulster Constabulary.

HAMC – Durham

In February 1981, a Task Force was set established to investigate the illegal drug activities of the Hells Angels Motorcycle Club in Durham. Representatives from the Durham County Sheriff's Office, ALE, SBI, FBI, and ATF were assigned to the task force. The task force identified the members, looked at their criminal records, attempted to cultivate informers (next to impossible), and conduct surveillance. In July, HAMC World Rally was held at Kerr Lake with members in attendance from all over the world. No arrests were made, but valuable intelligence was gathered that would prove very beneficial to law enforcement throughout the country.

Sixty-eight gallons of moonshine seized in the trunk of a car on US 1 and Gresham Lake Road in Raleigh, NC. Courtesy of Buzzy Anthony.

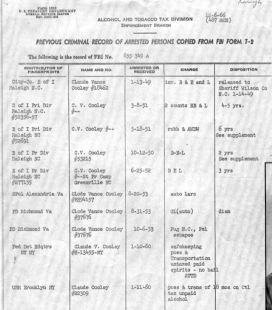

The arrest record of CV Cooley, December 1966. Inset: Arrest photograph of Claude Vance (CV) Cooley for possession and transportation of nontaxpaid liquor in New York, January 9, 1960.

Large still seized in Magnolia, NC, on October 2, 1973. Courtesy of Charlie Favre.

Mash boxes at the Magnolia raid. Courtesy of Charlie Favre.

The Magnolia still after being destroyed by explosives. Courtesy of Charlie Favre.

The News and Observer

Saturday, October 13, 1973   Raleigh, N.C.   Page 17

Still Raided; 5 Arrested

MAGNOLIA — Law officers raided a 17,000-gallon moonshine whisky still in Duplin County Friday that was reportedly part of an illegal operation exporting liquor to northern states.

Ralph Ellis of Goldsboro, U. S. Treasury Department agent, said that federal, state and local authorities arrested five men in connection with the raid — four in Magnolia and one in Brooklyn, N. Y.

Three men — James Stricklandd, 30, of Rocky Mount, Roy Taylor, 45, of Rougemont and Carter Bland, 25, of Bailey — were arrested at the site of the still, four miles west of Magnolia.

Another man, George Maynard of Magnolia, operator of a hog farm on which the still was located, was arrested at 11 a.m. Friday. The agents allowed him to finish feeding and watering the hogs before placing him under arrest.

Maynard is principal of

James Kenan High School in Duplin County.

A fifth man, James Newkirk, 44, of Magnolia, was arrested by federal agents at 3:30 a.m. Friday in Brooklyn, N. Y. He was driving a truck which contained 42 gallons of nontax-paid whisky produced by the still, agents said.

Ellis said the still had been under observation for several days. He said it probably cost $15,000 to build. At the site were 38 330-gallon fermenting boxes and 26 110-gallon fermenting barrels. Hog feed was used as an ingredient for the mash, he said.

The still had a capacity of 17,000 gallons of mash and was producing about 600 gallons of whisky daily, Ellis said. When the raid was staged, 430 gallons of whisky had been bottled and readied for shipment. The still had operated

for less than a month.

The still will be destroyed by explosives, Ellis said.

Strickland, Taylor and Bland are being held in the Wayne County Jail, charged with possession of an illicit still and nontax-paid whisky. Maynard was charged with possession of an illicit still and nontax-paid whisky and with conspiring to operate a still.

Newkirk was charged with possession and transportation of illegal whisky and was to face arraignment before a U. S. magistrate in Brooklyn.

The raid was the result of a joint probe conducted by the Goldsboro office of the Alcohol, Tobacco and Firearms Division of the U. S. Department of the Treasury, the Duplin County Sheriff's Department and New Hanover County Alcoholic Beverage Control officers.

Leaf Estimates

Raleigh News and Observer article about a large still seized in Magnolia, NC, on October 12, 1973.

Barn in the farm in Marengo, IN, that housed a large moonshine still seized in January 1971. Courtesy of Ed Garrison.

Large moonshine still with 12,000 gallons of mash capacity located in the Marengo, IN, barn. Courtesy of Ed Garrison.

Marengo, IN, moonshine still. Courtesy of Ed Garrison.

Officers involved with the Marengo still seizure, names unknown but believed to be Indiana officers. Courtesy of Ed Garrison.

Ford pick-up truck loaded with 300 gallons of moonshine seized in Granville County in January 1971. The moonshine was transported from Wilkes County by Wayne Clay "Rooster" Miller, who was arrested. Courtesy of Buzzy Anthony.

A large distillery seized in Harnett County, NC, consisting of twenty 480-gallon submarine stills and 8,100 gallons of mash. Three moonshiners were arrested as they operated the still. Pictured l-r: ATF Agents Bob Furr and John Lorrick and Johnston County ABC Officer James Barefoot (background) and ATF Agent Ronnie Williams.

Still seized in a garage in Harnett County. Pictured is ATF Agent Gene Calcote. Courtesy of Charlie Favre.

Concrete building inside a fenced hog lot in the Sutton area of Franklin County, NC.

ATF Agent Johnny Binkley and a steam still seized on March 25, 1972 located inside the concrete building in Franklin County.

Mash barrels at the hog lot. Pictured l-r: ATF Agent Johnny Binkley, Franklin County Deputy Arthur Johnson, ATF Agent Chuck Stanfill, Franklin County Sheriff William Dement, and Franklin County Deputies Lloyd Gupton, Leroy Terrell, and Vernon Scarboro.

Newspaper article and photos related to the Hot Lot still seizure. Pictured top right, l-r: Franklin County Deputies Arthur Johnson and David Batton, Sheriff William Dement, and ATF Area Supervisor Herb Steely. Pictured bottom left are Deputy Gupton and Area Supervisor Steely. Courtesy of The Franklin Times.

169

ry 11, 1

Officers Nab Still , Arrest Three Men

Scene above shows law officers viewing the site of a 4800-gallon capacity whiskey still, captured Wednesday near Royal. Shown, left to right are: Johnny Binkley, local area ATF officer; Herbert Steely, Area ATF Supervisor and Franklin Sheriff William T. Dement. Two men, identified as Coy Macon Pleasants, w/m/28, and Spencer Duke Lowery, w/m/30, both of Route 1, Youngsville were arrested at the still. A third man, identified as Herman Foster, c/m/60, Route 1, Louisburg was arrested at his home nearby. The site of the operation was a few yards off the Flat Rock Road about one mile west of Royal. ATF agents Stephen Calcote and Bob Bowen discovered the still and made the arrests as part of a saturation coverage of the Franklin County area by federal officers. Captured at the site were four 1200-gallon stills; 216 gallons of whiskey; a 1960 model Comet automobile; 2,000 gallons of mash; 21 100-pound gas cylinders and other still equipment. The three arrested will face hearings in District Court here on February 7th.

-Staff photo by Clint Fuller.

Newspaper article related to the seizure of a large still in the Royal section of Franklin County, January 1972. The still consisted of four 1,200-gallon metal tanks and was in full operation at the time of discovery. Bud Lowery and Coy Pleasants Jr. were arrested. Picture l-r are ATF agents Johnny Binkley and Herb Steely. Courtesy of The Franklin Times.

Mobile home in the Merry Hill section of Bertie County, where four 4,500-gallon metal tank stills were seized with a mash capacity of 16,000 gallons, May 1972.

Add-on room at the rear of the Bertie County mobile home.

4500-gallon metal tank stills in Bertie County.

Stills being dismantled and removed.

ATF Agents (l-r) Don Torrence, Henry Byrd, and Phil McGuire.

Sign directing onlookers to the Merry Hill distillery.

Still seized in the Flat Rock Church section of Franklin County on June 20, 1972. Pictured l-r: ATF Agent Johnny Binkley, ATF Area Supervisor Herb Steely, ATF Agent Chuck Stanfill, and ATF Investigator-in-Charge Michael Zetts.

Large underground still seized in Cabarrus County, NC, 1968, consisting of 1,062-gallon stills capable of producing 600 gallons of moonshine daily. Courtesy of Phil Carter.

FORM 1537 (REV. AUGUST 1965)	DEPARTMENT OF THE TREASURY - INTERNAL REVENUE SERVICE **CHEMIST'S REPORT OF EXAMINATION OF SAMPLES** ALCOHOL AND TOBACCO TAX	IN REPLY REFER TO AT:L: CEP:1h

Atlanta, Georgia

Chief Special Investigator
Charlotte, North Carolina

December 18 , 19 70

Re: NC E-16317 (IL) State
Charles Ray Smith, et al
409 E. Lane Street
Raleigh, North Carolina

Dear Sir:

An examination has been made of one samples sent in by Johnny C. Binkley, Inv.

with letter of transmittal dated 11-16-70 Samples received: 11-17-70

Secured by Johnny C. Binkley, Inv. Samples taken: 11-12-70

Delivered by Parcel Post Samples analyzed:

Type of product submitted: Illicit Mash

Sample No.	Form 1492 or 3294 No.	Description
93492	75383	Whiskey Mash fit for Distillation.

% Alcohol by Volume - 9.70

Clarence E. Paul
Chief, Laboratory Branch

Analyst JW

FORM 1537 (REV. 8-65)

ATF Chemist's report on a mash sample that shows the alcholic content of the mash being 9.7% by volume.

Halifax County ABC Chief Garland Bunting and ATF Agent Ed Garrison at a Nash County still. Courtesy of Ed Garrison.

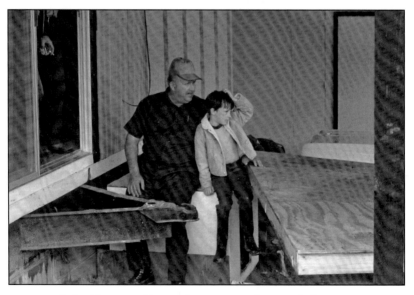

Garland Buntin and his son, Carey Bunting. Courtesy of Ed Garrison.

Homegoing Service
for
CAREY GARLAND BUNTING

April 23, 1926 - August 22, 1995

Scotland Neck Funeral Home
August 24, 1995
11:00 a.m.

Right: Funeral bulletin for the Carey Garland Bunting service. Courtesy of Charlie Favre.

Below: Obituary for Garland Bunting. Courtesy of Charlie Favre.

OBITUARY

Carey Garland Bunting was born in Oak City, N. C., to Dennis Earl Bunting and Reba Elnora Lynch Bunting. His law enforcement career which spanned fifty years, began in Oak City, where he was the town's policeman. An army veteran of Company A 175th Military Battalion, he served in the Korean War. Upon discharge he returned to North Carolina where he resumed his law enforcement career working as an under-cover agent with the state for several years. He was the Halifax County ABC officer for 35 years.

Garland is the subject of a book entitled *Moonshine* which was published in 1985. It tells of some of his experiences. He was featured in several local, state, and national newspapers and magazines. Also, he appeared in television documentaries on the state and national levels as well as being a guest on local radio and national television. His life story has been written and is being produced for the movie screen.

Garland loved people and was known for his knack for story telling. He enjoyed being the bright spot in a person's day. A 32nd degree Mason, he was a member of Skewarkee Lodge #90 in Williamston and Scottish Rite Bodies in New Bern, N.C.

In 1982 the Alcohol, Tobacco, and Firearms branch of the federal government presented him with the prestigious "Gallatin" award.

Garland was preceded in death by his son Carey Jackson Bunting. Surviving are his wife of thirty-four years, Helen Colleen Murray Bunting, of the home; a daughter, Joan Annette Bunting, of New Orleans, Louisiana; and a sister, Eileen B. Pate, of Tarboro, N.C.

Salisbury ATF Agents Bob Martin and Bruce Bassett on surveillance. Courtesy of Bill Belvin.

Salisbury ATF Agents Bob Martin and John Spidell with local officers destroying a large still. Courtesy of Bill Belvin.

THE SECRETARY OF THE TREASURY
WASHINGTON 20220

SEP 17 1974

Dear Rex:

A rumor was brought to my attention a few days ago regarding the parcelling out of the regulatory and enforcement functions at ATF. I am unable to find any substance for it, and can definitely advise you that no such recommendation has been received by the Treasury Department.

I am dismayed that the Government rumor mill can generate such disquieting, morale destroying and counterproductive talk. Although it is difficult to trace down and lay to rest something that we cannot put our fingers on, please be assured that we at Treasury look forward to many more years of able administration by ATF of the alcohol, tobacco and firearms laws and regulations.

Sincerely,

William E. Simon

Mr. Rex D. Davis
Director
Bureau of Alcohol,
 Tobacco and Firearms
Department of the Treasury
Washington, D. C. 20226

Letters from the Secretary of Treasury and ATF Director to employees concerning transfer of ATF functions in 1974. Printed in the ATF Newsletter, September 1974.

SPECIAL MESSAGE from the Director
Bureau of Alcohol, Tobacco and Firearms
Washington, D.C.

September 19, 1974

To My Associates in ATF:

Recently, there have been widespread rumors concerning a proposal to transfer the functions of the Bureau of Alcohol, Tobacco and Firearms into various other organizations. Due to the unusual pervasiveness of these rumors and their adverse impact on employee morale, I asked the Department of the Treasury for reassurance as to the organizational integrity of ATF.

I know the attached letter from Secretary Simon will put to rest any apprehensions you may have concerning the future of our organization. The letter is indicative also of the understanding and support we receive from the Department of the Treasury.

Let us now justify the confidence of the Department in ATF by turning our full attention to effectively discharging our many important responsibilities.

Rex D. Davis

Rex D. Davis
Director

Attachment

ranklin Times

Serving All Of Franklin County

LOUISBURG, N.C., THURSDAY, MARCH 7, 1974   (12 PAGES TODAY)   106 YEARS NUMBER 5

Two Charged In Liquor Raid

Federal and county law enforcement officials arrested two men at a liquor still on Tuesday night near the Cascine Plantation south of Louisburg.

The men were arrested as an old farmhouse as they were loading cases of white liquor on a pickup truck.

Franklin County Sheriff William Dement said Glenn Wade Whitley, 41, of Route 5, Louisburg and Johnnie Daniel Allen, 32, of Southport were charged with possession and manufacture of non-taxpaid whiskey and jailed in lieu of $2,500 bond each. The men posted bond and were released Wednesday afternoon after bond was reduced to $1,000 each.

The farmhouse contained two 480-gallon stills, 17 220-gallon mash barrels, 12 110-gallon mash barrels, and a large assortment of other equipment, raw materials, and containers. The cooker featured two gas burners fueled by bottled propane. An elaborate arrangement of hoses and electric pumps carried the mash into the still and provided water to cool the cooker. The still featured a 3-foot copper condenser.

In addition to 108 gallons of whiskey found at the farmhouse, officers discovered 954 gallons (155 cases) in a mobile home on S.R. 1110 about three miles from the still. The home was owned by Whitley.

Federal Alcohol, Tobacco and Firearm Agent Herb Steely estimated the operation was producing 300 gallons per day. The tax fraud on the liquor found in the mobile home was estimated at $22,560. Steely said illicit whiskey usually bought $6 a gallon and that the 954 gallons in the mobile home would likely have sold for about $6,000.

Officers poured out the liquor found in the mobile home and destroyed the whiskey and nonsalvageable materials found at the still. Sheriff Dement said the arrests followed a week of surveillance work by federal and county officers.

Causby Speaks At District VI Meeting

The annual meeting of District VI of the North Carolina State School Boards Association was held at Louis

Pruette Elected To Top Post

C. Ray Pruette, Past District Governor, Lions International, was elected President of the North Carolina Association for the Blind at its third quarterly meeting held in Raleigh Saturday.

June 8, 1974 in Charlotte, N. C. He will represent over 16,000 Lions in 440 Lions Clubs in the 100 counties of North Carolina.

Above: Newspaper article on the seizure of a large still and moonshine at the Cascine Plantation on March 6, 1974. Pictured top are Sheriff Dement and ATF Supervisor Herb Steely. At bottom are ATF Agent Don Devaney and Sheriff Dement. Courtesy of The Franklin Times.

Right: Officers destroying 954 gallons of moonshine located in a mobile home near a large distillery seized at the Cascine Plantation on March 6, 1974. Standing l-r are ATF Agent Johnny Binkley and Sheriff Dement; kneeling is ATF Supervisor Herb Steely.

Unique tomb cemetery located on US 401 in Franklin County.

NC ATF pistol team after winning the Southeast Regional Pistol Match, 1974. Pictured l-r: Bob Powell, Charlie Mercer, Bill Behen, Ken London, Ronnie Williams, and Roger Brown. From the November 1974 issue of the ATF Newsletter.

North Carolina State Bureau of Investigations (SBI) Agent Joe Hines destroying explosive devices.

182

THE
SOUTHEASTERNER

APRIL 1976

EMPLOYEE NEWSLETTER   BUREAU OF ALCOHOL, TOBACCO & FIREARMS   DEPARTMENT OF THE TREASURY

COMMENTS FROM MR. PIPER

ARD CRIMINAL ENFORCEMENT

When invited to write an article for the "Southeasterner", I found it difficult to write on one topic which would be of interest to all ATF employees in the Southeast Region. With the massive enforcement effort in the Southeast, which is about twice the size of any other enforcement operation in the United States, it becomes difficult to spend much time thinking of ATF as a whole, or of any of the other many functions in ATF which contribute to its overall operation.

It seems that in the last four years, Criminal Enforcement has been in a constant state of change, with Operation CUE (Concentrated Urban Enforcement) being the most recent upheaval, since it requires us to furnish 46 Special Agents to Chicago, Illinois.

Along with CUE, I would like to point up some of the changes that have taken place in the Southeast Region in the past three years. Out of seven Special Agents in Charge, only two of the original seven

are left. We have seven (out of seven) new Assistant Special Agents in Charge. With the exception of three positions, the entire regional Criminal Enforcement staff has changed. Along with massive transfers of supervisory positions throughout the Bureau, the Special Agent staffing in the Southeast Region has been reduced by over 150 positions. The diabolical FTS telephone system has now been refined to the point where you can dial numbers anywhere in the U. S., including off-net numbers. Our Headquarters now has FTS automatic dialing, where they can dial a total of 31 telephone numbers which have been programmed into the telephone, but pushing two buttons.

Our entire Criminal Enforcement system is geared to the computer, where unique identifiers identify any case with the speed of light. We can hit the San Diego computer, then to Washington, back to San Diego, and back to the requesting office as fast as the TECS Clerk can lift her fingers from the machine. Time breakdowns by enforcement category and the entire enforcement spectrum on a criminal case, such as prosecutions, sentences, etc., can be obtained in minutes. The old "daily report of investigator" is now a computer card.

I point all of this out merely to show what has happened to ATF in the last four years. All of this sophisticated equipment is only as good as the Special Agents who use it. In order to make all of this work; in order to justify the particular RAIC office in a given area; the central District Office in your state; the Regional Office of Atlanta, Bureau Headquarters, it all hinges on the fact that a Special Agent gets in an old Government car, perfects a criminal case, drives out and puts the handcuffs on a violator. Don't ever forget that factor.

The ATF Southeasterner (Southeast Region) employee newsletter for January 1976. Courtesy of Neta Rice

STATE OF NORTH CAROLINA

OFFICE OF THE GOVERNOR

RALEIGH 27611

JAMES B. HUNT, JR.
GOVERNOR

MEMORANDUM

TO: Johnny Binkley, Special Agent, U.S. Bureau of Alcohol, Tobacco
                                                        and Firearms

FROM: Gov. James B. Hunt, Jr.

RE: Cigarette Smuggling

DATE: June 12, 1979

      Cigarette smuggling is a crime with serious implications
in North Carolina, and my administration is strongly committed
to doing everything possible to aid the anti-smuggling efforts
of law enforcement officers in North Carolina and other states.

      It is particularly important that the Department of
Revenue, which is responsible for administering the cigarette
tax and licensing wholesale distributors, give whatever assistance
it can in this regard. This assistance must, of course, take into
account the department's responsibility to collect all state
taxes and the department's limited budget and personnel.

      I am asking you to appoint a representative of the
U.S. Bureau of Alcohol, Tobacco and Firearms to meet with a
representative of my office and discuss ways in which the Department
of Revenue can give this assistance. I would aks this task force
group to prepare appropriate recommendations for my consideration
as quickly as possible. The State Bureau of Investigation,
the State Highway Patrol, the Department of Revenue and the U.S.
Bureau of Alcohol, Tobacco and Firearms will be represented on
this task force.

      I am asking my Press Secretary, Gary Pearce, to coordinate
this group's study. He will contact the representatives of your
departments individually and then convene the group by the end of
this week to discuss possible recommendations.

###

*Memorandum from NC Governor James B. Hunt to ATF Agent Johnny Binkley setting forth his commitment to anti-smuggling efforts and requesting the establishment of a task force to address the cigarette smuggling problem. **Inset:** UPI newspaper article reporting the seizure of contraband cigarettes and arrests of three individuals in New York, 1978.*

Cigarette raid nets over 6,000 cartons

WASHINGTON (UPI) — Treasury Department agents seized 6,250 cartons of cigarettes in New York Thursday and arrested three suspected smugglers in a drive against "kingpins and couriers of a multimillion-dollar racket."

G.R. Dickerson, director of the department's Bureau of Alcohol, Tobacco and Firearms, said none of the cigarettes seized had the required New York tax stamp, indicating no levy was paid on them.

The bureau said Andon Gudrupis, 30, and Jack Scelzo, 22, both of New York, were arrested in Tottenville, N.Y., with 5,000 cartons of cigarettes. Walter Howard, 46, of Englishtown, N.J., was arrested in Brooklyn with 1,250 cartons.

All three were charged with violating a New York law banning possession of cigarettes that are not stamped.

DEPARTMENT OF THE TREASURY
BUREAU OF ALCOHOL, TOBACCO AND FIREARMS
222 So. Church St., Suite 404
Charlotte, North Carolina 28202
February 9, 1979

REFER TO
C:NC:JCW:ah
3270.9A

MEMORANDUM TO: All Resident Agents in Charge

FROM: Special Agent in Charge

SUBJECT: Manpower Expenditures

The first quarter CARS printout of FY-1979 shows that North Carolina special agents are expending excessive manhours on the illicit liquor program.

Keeping in mind that illicit liquor is the Bureau's last priority, I am requesting that each Resident Agent in Charge take a closer look at his special agents' activities where related to illicit liquor.

There will be no more manhours expended on illicit liquor unless an agent has <u>very reliable</u>, <u>specific</u> information on the location of a distillery with a utilized mash capacity in excess of <u>1,000 gallons</u>.

There will be no further time expended on walk-through or fly-through <u>operations of any type</u>.

There will be no further time expended on contacting informers for illicit whiskey information <u>only</u>.

Informer contact should be directed toward gathering information on Explosives, Firearms and Cigarette Smuggling, and so charged on the Time Application Report. Information solicited regarding illicit liquor should be incidental or secondary to these above stated Bureau priorities.

Please have all special agents initial this memorandum and return a copy to the District Office immediately.

John C. Westra

Charlotte SAC memo to all agents that illicit liquor is ATF's last priority and setting manpower limitations on illicit liquor investigations.

Johnny C. Binkley

DEPARTMENT OF THE TREASURY
BUREAU OF ALCOHOL, TOBACCO AND FIREARMS
WASHINGTON, D.C. 20226

MAY 17 1982   REFER TO

MEMORANDUM TO: All Employees (Criminal Enforcement)

      FROM: Assistant Director (Criminal Enforcement)

   SUBJECT: Notification of Reduction-in-Force

Because a final decision regarding the supplemental appropriations
for the Bureau of Alcohol, Tobacco and Firearms has not been reached,
it is necessary to issue a new notification of reduction-in-force.
The notice, dated February 1, 1982, is hereby cancelled and this
memorandum shall serve as general notification that it may be necessary
to conduct a reduction in force, including the possibility of furloughing
employees. Although we do not yet know what all of the individual
actions will be, we believe that some employees may be reassigned,
demoted, separated, or furloughed for more than 30 days.

At this time we do not know whether you will be able to remain in
your present position, or if some other action will affect your
employment. No personnel action will be taken any earlier than
30 days following your receipt of this notice. You will receive
a specific notice not later than 10 working days before the effective
date of any personnel action to be taken in your case.

We want to assure you that all decisions affecting your employment
will be made in accordance with your rights under reduction-in-force
regulations. If you disagree with the action taken, you should not
file an appeal to the Merit Systems Protection Board until the day
after the effective date of the personnel action. You will then have
20 calendar days after the effective date of the action to file an
appeal with the MSPB or 30 days to file a discrimination complaint
with the Bureau's EO Office. More detailed information on filing
procedures will be included in a specific notice.

This notice expires August 21, 1982. If we have not given you a more
specific notice stating the action to be taken, or if we have not
extended this expiration date on or before August 21, 1982, this
notice will expire and you may disregard it.

for Robert E. Sanders

Received (Signature)   Date   5-25-82

---

*Memorandum to All Employees (Criminal Enforcement) from Assistant Director (Criminal Enforcement)…
Subject: Notification of Reduction-in-Force.*

Taken at a public school building in Greensboro, NC, April 1980, while Ronald Reagan was campaigning for President of the United States. Agent David McAleer was standing post at the exit door for Reagan's departure. He was looking into the sun and President Reagan notice the grimace on his face and said, "Don't worry, it will get better in November...nice tie!" The photograph was taken by the parents of one of the secret service agents, who later sent McAleer a copy. McAleer later sent the photograph and an explanation of the circumstances to the White House. A few weeks later he received the photograph back signed by President Reagan during his stay in the hospital following his unscheduled meeting with Mr. John Hinkley on the sidewalk of the Hilto Hotel in D.C. Courtesy of David McAleer

ATF Agents Newt Plemmons and Neal Crisp enjoying the sights in New York City during a United Nations detail in 1985.

187

Raleight ATF agents examining and processing seized firearms. Pictured l-r: ATF Agents Dave McAleer, Johnny Binkley, and David Lazar. Courtesy of David McAleer.

Members of the Raleigh Fire Department put out a fire at the Sparkles Night Club, Hodges Street, February 25, 1985. Courtesy of the Raleigh Fire Department.

director's memorandum

"Dedicated to Excellence"

BUREAU OF ALCOHOL, TOBACCO AND FIREARMS/DEPARTMENT OF THE TREASURY   DECEMBER 1988

NRA Seeks Judgment Against ATF

by Jack Patterson
Assistant Chief Counsel
(Firearms & Explosives)

On September 29, 1988, a civil complaint was filed in the U.S. District Court, Charleston, South Carolina, by the National Rifle Association (NRA) and eight other plaintiffs seeking an injunction against the enforcement by ATF of certain firearms regulations implementing the Gun Control Act of 1968, as amended.

At issue are the definition of "manufacture" (which includes the term after), the definition of "business premises" for purposes of licensing under the Act, recordkeeping requirements for licensees' transactions in personal guns, and the definition of gun shows at which licensees may conduct their firearms business.

The plaintiffs seek a declaratory judgment that the regulations are invalid due to the Bureau's alleged failure to follow the requirements of the Administrative Procedures Act with regard to holding a public hearing. They also request an injunction against enforcement of the regulations on the basis that irreparable harm will result if they are enforced.

A hearing on the law suit was scheduled for December 12. ∎

McGuire Retires

As Associate Director for Law Enforcement, Phillip C. McGuire headed ATF criminal enforcement programs and investigations for the past 6 years. During this period, ATF had a greater impact and became more visible in the areas of firearms enforcement, bombing investigations, and major arson cases. The following contains excerpts from an October interview with McGuire on his retirement from ATF after 26 years as a special agent.

Q: How has the agency changed since you came on as the youngest ATF agent?

A: You're right that when I became an ATF agent I was the youngest agent with ATF (23 years old). That in itself is significant to point out the changes. We have many agents today that we hire at that age or a little bit younger. The changes have been much greater than that. When I became an agent I was sworn in on May 7, 1962, in Aiken, South Carolina, and for all practical purposes we were very much a single jurisdiction agency with primary responsibility for protecting the revenue from illicit liquor manufacturers.

But ATF changed dramatically over the years, specifically in 1968 when the Gun Control Act was passed and we hired a lot of new agents. Then with the passage of the Explosives Control Act of 1970 we made major changes. We progressed further in our expertise in firearms and explosives, and then in the early 80's, with the passage of the Cigarette Smuggling Act, we took on additional responsibility. So ATF has
Continued on page 6.

Compliance Names Award After Shoemaker

by Audrey Stucko
Program Development & Monitoring Section

Recently Compliance Operations initiated a leadership award for newly hired employees who attend Basic Training classes. The purpose of the award is to recognize individuals who demonstrate leadership qualities and exemplify the characteristics of a model employee while attending CO Basic Training.

The award is named after the late Larry N. Shoemaker. Larry, as many of you know, volunteered and taught in numerous Basic Training classes while assigned as an inspector to the San Antonio office. A better role model would be difficult, if not impossible, to find.
Continued on page 4.

Photograph and article on the retirement of Phil McGuire, Assistant Director of Law Enforcement. From the ATF Director's Memorandum, December 1988 edition.

Retirement party announcement for ATF Agent Pat Kelly, Glynco, GA.

189

Special Agent-In-Charge Paul Lyon presenting an award at the Raleigh ATF office. Pictured l-r: Agents Ed Garrison, Dave McAleer, Ron Tunkel, Johnny Binkley, Earl Woodham, Chuck Stanfill, Paul Lyon, Ken Brady, Sam Lewis, and Bill Marshall.

Raleigh ATF POD personnel, 1990. Pictured l-r: Bill Marshall, Ed Garrison, Ken Brady, Ruth Strickland, Ron Tunkel, Synthia Kearney, Johnny Binkley, and Dave McAleer.

ATF golfers at a Myrtle Beach golf outing, ca. 1991.

Explosive Incidents

In addition to the cigarette and firearms cases, incidences of misuse of explosives became more prevalent. Information was received that a number of teenagers in the Cary area had broken into an explosives storage facility and stole a large quantity of explosives, and were attempting to sell them. Our investigation identified the teens involved and the recovery of several pounds of commercial explosives and blasting caps. After identifying the leader of the group, we went to his home to interview him. He denied any involvement and his mother, of course very protective of her son, was somewhat hostile and defiant as to our presence. However, after the boy admitted he had the explosives and showed us where they were concealed under the flooring in his bedroom, she had a change of heart and turned her hostility away from us to the boy.

Chatham County Sheriff Jack Elkins requested assistance in the investigation and disposal of a case of old dynamite turned over to him by a farmer who claimed to have found the dynamite on his property. Special Agent Garrison and I interviewed Sheriff Elkins and the farmer who reiterated he had found the explosives near a bridge construction site. The dynamite was old and deteriorated and appeared to have been left out in the elements for quite some time. With no evidence to the contrary, we concluded that the dynamite had been left there by one of the construction companies that had worked on the bridge. We threw the case in the trunk of my car to carry to our storage location in Raleigh.

After about a week of driving around with the dynamite in the trunk, we remembered it was there and took it to the storage site at Nordan's Transportation. A few days later, we got a call from Nordan's that the dynamite was deteriorated to the point it was considered unsafe to store and asked us to pick it up. After a rather frantic search for some place to get rid of the dynamite, we contacted a large quarry east of Raleigh for assistance. They agreed to detonate the dynamite in connection with some blasting they were doing the next day.

In another incident, Raleigh officers Mike Longmire and A.C. Monday conducted a drug search in the Boylan section of Raleigh and found a blasting cap and a small amount of Tovex explosives. A joint investigation conducted with the Raleigh PD revealed that the

Tovex was part of a large explosives theft. We later determined that some of the stolen explosives had been carried to Florida, where the suspects tried to sell it. Unable to get rid of the explosives, the suspects returned to North Carolina and stashed it on a farm in Franklin County owned by one of the suspects. We recovered and destroyed 70 lbs of the Tovex explosives and arrested two suspects on federal charges.

Over a period of several weeks, there were a rash of called- in bomb threats at various state government buildings in Raleigh. While it was assumed that the threats were hoaxes, the buildings had to be evacuated and law enforcement called in to search and investigate. The responding agencies were usually the State Capital Police, SBI, Raleigh PD and ATF. No devices were ever found. After a while, it was realized that the threats were usually occurring on Fridays in the early afternoon. And since the investigations and searches took a few hours, the evacuated employees were not required to come back to work that day. Oddly enough, after the policy was changed to require the evacuated employees to remain in the area and return to work after the search the calls stopped

On one occasion during that period, a suspicious package was found in an office at the Highway Department building in downtown Raleigh. The building was evacuated and the usual agencies responded. Interviews with employees revealed that a brown paper bag had been found, and no one knew anything about it or how it had gotten there. At that time, other than military EOD, the SBI was the only agency trained and willing to deal with suspected explosives devices.

After SBI Agent Joe Hines arrived on the scene, it was somehow decided that he and I would enter the building to try to determine the nature of the suspicious package. Joe entered the building and then the office, as I followed at a very safe distance behind. After he opened the office door, we could see the suspicious package, the brown paper bag. Joe slowly and cautiously made his way over to and opened the bag and carefully pulled out its contents: a 3-pack of ladies underwear, size large. We later determined that one of the women in the office had brought them in to return to Belk's on her lunch hour. But she had to leave work early unexpectedly, and just forgot that she had left them behind her desk.

Chapter Fourteen
ATF SURVIVES AND MOVES ON (1982-1983)

S tephen E. Higgins was appointed ATF Director in March 1983, after serving a year as the acting director. Phil McGuire was appointed the Associate Director of Law Enforcement in 1982, and as such was the head of the criminal enforcement programs and investigations. Both were very experienced men, having worked their way up through the ranks. Mr. Higgins joined ATF in 1961 as an Inspector in Omaha, Nebraska and worked up through the ranks to Assistant Director for Regulatory Enforcement where he served from 1975 until 1982.

Mr. McGuire from Boone, North Carolina, joined ATF in 1962, serving as a Special Investigator in South Carolina and North Carolina. He was later promoted to Regional Investigator in Atlanta. As a Regional Investigator, McGuire worked undercover and major liquor investigations resulting in large liquor and still seizures throughout Tennessee and North Carolina. I knew Mr. McGuire by reputation and also having worked with him on several liquor investigations. He impressed me as very capable, hardworking, and one not afraid or above "getting on the ground".

The South Carolina District office was closed and the offices and agents were placed in the Charlotte Division—or North Carolina Division, as it was sometimes called. Some twelve years later when I retired, the annually published division personnel roster was still headed "North Carolina Division". Just another example of South Carolina having always to play second fiddle to the Old North State.

Abolish ATF

The "abolish ATF movement" resurfaced again after the election of President Reagan, who was viewed by many as pro-gun and anti-ATF. Unlike the abolish ATF rumors in 1974, this time it turned out to be more than mere rumor. In the fall of 1981, the

Washington Post ran a story headlined that ATF was going to be abolished. And then in May 1982, I, along with all others, received an official "Notice of Reduction in Force" letter outlining the process and procedures that would take place with the abolishment of the agency. About the same time, at a district firearms qualification in Fayetteville, the ASAC announced that the abolishment of the agency was a done deal and that "some" agents would be absorbed by the Secret Service. Shortly thereafter, the local Secret Service supervisor made inquiry regarding the inventory of desk and office equipment as well as government cars.

Of course, the rumors were rampant about the proposed abolishment of ATF and what would happen to the laws enforced by ATF, and more importantly what was going to be the fate of the agents and support personnel. The general consensus was that the explosives laws and some firearms jurisdiction would go to the FBI, the remainder of the firearms laws and some agents would go over to the Secret Service, and the liquor laws and some personnel might go to Customs.

The "some agents" who would go to the Secret Service and possibly to Customs was the cause of consternation, especially with the newly hired agents (last hired, first fired) and some older agents who had come on during the liquor days when a college degree was not required. Some of the newly hired agents, recognizing the last hired first fired, left ATF and went with other agencies, primarily US Customs. Some of the older agents who were eligible simply retired. But for most of us it was wait and speculate. To be honest, there were some agents who welcomed the idea of going to the Secret Service. They felt it was a more prestigious job and that pay grades and opportunities for promotion would be better. But I would say for the most part, agents were opposed to the idea. Then there was a period of no new information, no new rumors, and nothing. After what seemed like forever, the rumor spread that the "done deal" abolishment plan was dead, and we subsequently we received notification that it would not occur and cancelation of the Reduction in Force Letter.

Just what happened of course was never known for sure at the agent level, but most of us came to understand and believe the following scenario. The NRA and other pro-gun folks were not happy with the passage of the Gun Control Act of 1968 and were particularly unhappy with ATF enforcement and regulation. They felt that ATF was too strict, and often heavy-handed in dealing with licensed dealers and gun folks in general.

The so-called Ballew case in Maryland became a rallying point for the NRA and pro-gun folks. Ballew was shot and partially paralyzed during the execution of a search warrant by ATF and local officers. Ballew claimed he was in the shower and did not hear the agents knock and identify themselves. And when he got out of the shower, he heard the commotion in an adjoining room and came out with a gun. Seeing the gun, one of the local officers felt threatened and shot Ballew. Although a very controversial incident, a federal judge subsequently ruled that the agents acted reasonable and prudent.

The NRA and Pro-gun folks were able to convince the Reagan people and many in Congress that the abolishment of ATF was the right thing to do, and the plans were made to do just that. Then, as the plan moved ahead, some of the pro-gun folks started to take a little closer look at the situation and what the resulting effect might be. While they disliked the GCA of 1968 and ATF's enforcement, they started to realize that things might, in fact, be worse for them if the abolishment went through. They probably had accepted that the GCA of 1968 would not be repealed and would remain the law of the land as it related to firearms. But through their friends in the administration, the Congress, and the industry, they knew they could exercise some influence and control as to just how ATF regulated and enforced the law. On the other hand, if the firearms laws went to the FBI and Justice Department, their influence might be less and the enforcement and regulations might become more stringent. Furthermore, they may have theorized that if some of the firearms laws went to the Secret Service along with the ATF agents and an anti-gun President was elected, he would probably be able to push that anti-gun agenda through with the close ties to the Secret Service.

Some, or none, of the above may have occurred, but for whatever reason the ATF abolishment was squashed and just went away. Ironically, under the Reagan administration, ATF's budget increased significantly and it turned out that the administration was a strong supporter of ATF.

In spite of all the abolishment talk and the obvious distractions, we continued to work investigations and make cases. The Charlotte District and Raleigh POD, in particular, continued to work on cigarette smuggling. Although the results and anticipated level of smuggling activity had lessened significantly, we were still seeing some smuggling activity, usually in small amounts, from North Carolina going to the high-tax loss states. In most of the instances, we would relay the information to agents and officers in those states, conduct surveillance of the vehicles into Virginia, and then turn the investigation over to them. We (SAC Westra, SA Garrison, and me) were still involved in preparing and conducting Tobacco Enforcement training classes for state and local officers at FLETC.

Arson Laws

In addition to tobacco enforcement, Raleigh agents continued to work firearms, explosives, and arson investigations. ATF had recently expanded its jurisdiction for arson investigation under statute authority under the GCA of 1968 and the Organized Crime Control Act of 1970 (Explosive Law). Title II of the GCA of 1968 prohibits the manufacture, possession and use of destructive devices, and Title XI of the Organized Control Act made it a federal violation to use explosives to destroy certain types of property.

ATF took the position that when certain destructive devices and explosives (Molotov cocktails, a hot plate connected to combustible materials, etc.) were used it was, in fact, a violation of the Gun Control Act of 1968 and/or the Explosives Act of 1970. Deliberately set fires were most often set by merely igniting flammable liquids, such as gasoline with a match or lighted candle. It was ATF's assertion that gasoline mixed with air was a mechanical mixture that when ignited by fire caused an explosion, and thereby was a federal violation. Some courts agreed and ruled that it would be a violation, but some courts rejected the theory and ruled it was not. To resolve this problem, Title 18 USC, section 844, was amended by Public Law 97—298, to include language that specifically covered damage by fire. The amended law was commonly referred to as the Anti-Arson Act of 1982.

Tape City Arson Case

One of the first arson cases worked out of the Raleigh POD was initiated in January 1982, when a small strip shopping center building in Rocky Mount was destroyed by fire. The building, known as "Tape City", was partially destroyed in a fire one week prior to the fire that actually destroyed the building.

In the first fire, officers found several incendiary devices in the attic of the building that did not ignite and burn as designed. Local authorities contacted ATF for assistance in the investigation. Unlike some other federal agencies, ATF has always had good working relations with local and state officers. In the moonshine days we worked closely with local sheriffs, and local and state ABC officers. In firearms, explosives and tobacco investigations, we started working more closely with police departments, as well as the others. In arson investigations in particular, ATF and the SBI almost always partnered in conducting cause and origin, and follow up investigations.

An informal task force consisting of the SBI, Rocky Mount PD, Nash County Sheriff's Department, and ATF was established to investigate the Tape City fire. Later on, Steve Langham—a private insurance investigator—joined the team. We learned that the entire building, along with one of the shops within the building, was owned by Charles Langley and his brother. Charles Langley as previously noted (chapter 6) had been a major violator of the liquor laws and owner of large stills found in Indiana and North Carolina. Further, it was learned that just weeks before the fire Langley had just been released from state prison after serving a sentence for drug trafficking.

As in all arson fires, you must determine that it was in fact an intentionally set fire and establish a reason or motive for the fire. The discovery of the unconsumed incendiary devices in the first fire pretty much established that the fire was intentionally set. It was determined that the business was fully insured and in financial difficulty, thereby establishing the strong case that it was burned to collect the insurance.

Captain Milton Reams of the Nash County Sheriff's Office received information that an individual named Tommy was talking about the fire and how he was involved. We picked him up and he confessed to his limited involvement and identified the torch as being Billy. He said Billy actually set the fire, but he gave him a gas can and drove him to a gas station to buy gas and then dropped him off at the business. He stated that Billy returned to his home later and said he had set the fire and burned the building. A few days later we located Billy and interviewed him about the fire. He initially denied knowing anything about the fire, but after a few days in the Nash County Jail he wanted a deal. He confessed that Charles Langley paid him to finish the job after the first fire did not completely destroy the business. Billy and Tommy both agreed to testify regarding their involvement in the arson.

After a follow up investigation to corroborate their confessed activities, obtain financial records, and tie up other lose ends, Langley was brought in for questioning. Knowing how the game is played, he, of course, denied all the allegations and basically said you can go to hell. He was arrested and subsequently tried in Nash County Superior Court on three state felony charges relating to the burning of the building.

While none of us had any doubt as to Langley's guilt, as the trial date approached, I think we all started to have some concerns to the trial outcome. First of all, we all knew that the case would hinge on the testimony of Billy and Tommy, and whether or not they would be believed by the jury. Secondly, the judge in the case had been an up and coming young attorney in the Democratic Party who had been vetted for an appointment as the U.S. Attorney or possibly a federal bench appointment. During his background investigation, I understand something had been uncovered that took him out of consideration. Afterwards, he was appointed to the state bench and possibly would have some bias against the federal agents (the FBI had done his background). Thirdly, Langley had hired Jim Blackburn and Wade Smith, two of the most notable lawyers in the state. Blackburn was a former U.S. Attorney for the Eastern District of NC, whose claim to fame was that he successfully prosecuted Army Dr. Jeffrey MacDonald for killing his wife and two children at Ft. Bragg in 1970. Wade Smith was one of the most respected, successful, and sought-out attorneys in the state. (Ironically, Smith was on the Jeffrey MacDonald defense team when Blackburn prosecuted the case).

The trial lasted several days with the first few days devoted to establishing ownership of the property, admitting financial records, insurance information, and testimony from fire personnel as to what they did and found at the two fire scenes. While these procedures and evidence were necessary, we all knew the case would be won or lost on the testimony of Tommy and Billy. Their day came and both testified as to their knowledge and involvement in the burning of the building. Blackburn and Smith objected several times during their testimony and, of course, really went after them on cross examination. They both held their ground and maintained their testimony was true.

After summations, the case went to the jury. After several hours of deliberations, the jury returned a verdict of guilty on all counts. I was somewhat surprised, as was many in the courtroom not the least being Langley and his attorneys. The judge sentenced Langley to a term of ten years in the North Carolina Department of Corrections. His attorneys immediately gave notice of appeal and asked the judge to continue Langley's pre-trial release on bond pending the outcome of the appeal. The surprises continued, as the judge denied the request to continue the bond and ordered the defendant to be taken into custody immediately and transported to prison to begin his sentence. I must say, the trial and outcome reinforced my faith in the system.

Tommy and Billy were given assistance in relocating away from the Rocky Mount area, as it was felt there might be a possibility of retaliation resulting from their testimony. Langley's associates were able to locate Billy and attempted to get him to recant his testimony. Unknown to them, Billy was continuing to cooperate, and all their meetings and conversations were recorded. While the case progressed to the point of possible charges, the State and Federal prosecutors felt it would be a difficult case to try and recommended the investigation be dropped. In reflecting back, I think that was the right decision. Charles Langley died in March 2001.

HAMC – Ralph L

A firearms investigation was opened on Ralph L., a reputed member of the Durham HAMC. Information was developed that Ralph L., a convicted felon, was living in Wake County and had several firearms including a sawed-off shotgun in his residence. Through surveillance and information gathered from sources, we were able to obtain a federal search warrant for his residence. With assistance from the Wake County Sheriff's Department and the SBI, we executed the search warrant at his residence and seized nine guns. Ralph L. was home at the time of the search and was arrested for violation of the federal firearms laws — receipt and possession of a firearm by a convicted felon. He was convicted in Federal court and sentenced to a term in federal prison.

In one of those "what the hell were we thinking" times, our execution of the search warrant and arrest was questionable. Bob Graham and I walked up to Ralph L.'s residence, a mobile home, with me on one side of the door and Bob on the other. Graham announced our presence and that we had a search warrant. Ralph L. opened and filled the door with a vicious pit bull between his legs that he held back as it struggled to get to us. We asked him to step back and we entered the mobile home, at which time I observed guns hanging in holsters on each side of the door easily within his grasp. He could have easily shot us through the side of the mobile home or door when he opened it. This was back before the Special Response Teams (SRT), when you pretty much served your own search warrants and made your own arrests. To this day when I look back, I cringe at that and some other actions that we took. I reckon we just didn't know any better.

In 1983, the Planters Oil Mill in Rocky Mount was destroyed by a massive fire and we were called for assistance in the case. This case was significant in that it was the first case where the National Response Team (NRT) was called in for a Raleigh investigation. After a long exhaustive examination of the scene, the NRT found evidence of a flammable liquid but was unable to make a call on whether the fire was set accidentally or intentionally.

Chapter Fifteen
U.S. SECRET SERVICE DETAIL

ATF and other Treasury agencies (Customs, IRS) are often called upon to provide assistance to the US Secret Service in their Presidential candidate protective operations. The need, of course, is more during the Presidential primary and election period every four years. Agents are assigned to protective details for the President, Vice President, Presidential candidates and /or their families. Agents are primarily assigned to Post-Stander details, Residence Security details, or to Jump Team details. Post-stander details are usually for short periods, while the protectee is at a particular function, usually within the assigned area of the detailed agents.

For example, if the President attended a function in Raleigh, the Raleigh ATF agents and others from the Charlotte District, as needed, would be assigned to the detail. A post-stander, as the name implies, usually stands a post at some assigned location where the protectee will be visiting. It can range from an all-night detail watching the plane at the airport, to assigned points along the motorcade route to the event, or at the particular event location where the protectee will be attending. The post can be indoors and outdoors, sometimes a good post and often a not so good post perhaps in the rain or cold.

Residence Security details as the name implies entails assignment to a team that provides security for the candidate's residence. These assignments are for longer periods of time and to my knowledge, ATF is seldom called upon for these details. Assignment to a Jump Team detail is the third area in which ATF agents may be assigned. Jump Team details are usually for a long period of time requiring constant travel. Jump Teams keep moving ahead of the candidate to set up and provide security at a particular location, and then after the event jumps ahead to provide security the next candidate visit. Most ATF agents at one time or another were assigned

203

to Post-Standing details, but few were ever detailed to Residential Security or Jump Team assignments.

In September 1984, I was assigned to a Jump Team to provide security for the President, Vice-President, the Presidential candidate and Vice-Presidential candidate for the remaining campaign until the election in November. I was a little apprehensive, but excited about the assignment. I had heard stories that ATF and other non-Secret Service agents in prior years felt that they were treated badly on some details. They complained that they were given all the bad assignments (outside in cold and rain, long shifts) and less than desirable lodging arrangements.

Also, a sore spot with some was that the Secret Service referred to ATF and other non-Secret Service agents as OTA (Other Treasury Agents). I was assigned to Jump Team #69, one of fifteen teams put together to work the candidate security until the election in November. My team and the others were comprised of fifteen to sixteen agents with designated Team Leader. My team was comprised of three ATF agents, one Customs agent and one IRS agent, with the remainder being USSS agent. Other than me, the ATF agents were Roger Brewer, Birmingham, and Dick Stoltz out of the Reno office. The Team Leader was Dave Clark, a USSS agent out of Dallas.

On September 29, 19849, I flew from RDU to Cleveland, Ohio, for my first meeting with the team and our first assignment the following day. The event was the visit of Vice President Bush and Mrs. Bush at the Cleveland area Republican Party Picnic at the German Central Farm in Parma, Ohio. My assignment was to a vehicle in the motorcade and, sure enough, on the Site Post Assignment Log there was my name and "OTA" designation. It really didn't bother me. Vice President Bush (call name Timber Wolf) arrived in the afternoon, attended the event, and departed shortly before 6:00 pm. From my perspective, everything went well.

On October 1, 1984, we flew from Cleveland to Brownsville, Texas for a campaign visit by President Reagan (call name Rawhide) the following day. President Reagan attended a rally at Southmost College in the afternoon and then departed. The Team was scheduled to stay over that night, but I had to fly back home to attend my wife's grandmother's (Granny Fields) funeral. I found out that it was not easy getting from Brownsville, Texas to Bonlee, North Carolina on short notice, but I made it back via Houston, Atlanta, Charlotte, and Raleigh. On October 4, 1984—a Sunday—along with other Raleigh agents, I was assigned to a security detail for foreign dignitary attending a function at St. Augustine College in Raleigh.

On October 7th, I rejoined the team and we flew to Louisville, Kentucky, for the debate between the President and Presidential candidate Walter Mondale. The debate was held at the Kentucky Center for the Arts. I had a good assignment, as my post was stage right. The President and Mrs. Reagan stayed overnight in Louisville and departed the following morning.

The following morning at 5:00 am, we boarded an Air Force cargo plane (C-130, I believe) and flew to Baltimore for our next assignment. That was quite an experience, as we were on the plane with the Presidential limousine and other cargo with very little space. It was the first of two flights during the detail that we did not fly commercial. Later that day, President Reagan arrived and spoke at the Columbus Statue. I was posted with a Baltimore Police Officer on the rooftop of a building near the site to do crowd surveillance. A good assignment and one that really gave a good insight to the extensive and complicated planning and preparation that goes into a Presidential visit, especially an outside, open to the public event as this was.

On October 9th, we traveled by Amtrak from Baltimore to Philadelphia for the debate between Vice President Bush and Congresswoman Ferraro. The debate sponsored by the League of Women Voters was held at the Convention Center. The debate was on the 11th, but we stayed in Philadelphia until the 13th for some reason. One of the highlights was that I saw Mickey Mantle, my boyhood hero, at the hotel where we were staying. On October 13th, we departed Philadelphia to Greenville, South Carolina, for a visit in Greenville by President Reagan.

On October 16th, we flew to Atlanta to standby for our next assignment. We were initially designated to fly to Portland, Oregon, but just before boarding the flight we were reassigned to fly to New York for a Presidential visit. We were lodged at the Grand Hyatt Hotel next to the Grand Central Station.

I recall the hotel lobby was very large and impressive, with two or three small bars. My room, however, was very small with barely enough room for the bed and a dresser with little space to walk. But, I wasn't paying for it, and what can you expect for $165 (government rate, I presume) a night in New York City.

We were there for four days covering a couple functions attended by the President. The primary function was a dinner for the President at the Waldorf Astoria Hotel. My post was on the rooftop of the hotel along with a couple NYC Police officers. It was probably one of the most memorable assignments of the entire detail. The view was simply amazing with all the lights from the numerous surrounding buildings, and the noises and sounds of the street were fascinating—the honking of horns, chants from demonstrators below. The two New York City cops were very entertaining with their war stories from their experiences working in the city. Every time I see the opening scene of NYC on the Law and Order TV show I am reminded of that night.

On October 20th, we flew from New York to Los Angeles for a Presidential visit to the Rockwell International Test Installation in Palmdale, California. He toured an enormous hangar, where planes were at various stages of assembly. As I recall, the B-1 bomber was being assembled and tested at the time. On October 22nd, we flew to Atlanta and then to Columbus, Ohio for a Presidential visit to Ohio State University.

On October 24th, we drove to Cincinnati for a campaign visit by Vice President Bush. He spoke at a local high school and did a walking tour at Newport Steel.

On October 28th, we drove to Parkersburg, West Virginia for a visit by President Reagan. He rode in a high school parade and then spoke at a rally at the high school.

On October 29th, we departed Parkersburg and flew in the C-130 plane to Andrews Air Force base in Washington to standby for our next assignment.

On October 31st, we flew to Rochester, New York for a Presidential visit at the War Memorial Auditorium. I recall it was cold, rainy, and just gloomy weather.

On November 1st, we flew to Springfield, Illinois for a Presidential speech at the State Capital. There I caught one of my worst assignments—outside in the cold perimeter fence post at the airport.

On November 2nd, we traveled to St. Louis, Missouri by bus for visits by Presidential candidate Mondale and a visit by the President. Mr. Mondale made a visit to a local shopping mall, as I recall. The President arrived the following day for a speech and rally at the St. Louis Gateway Arch. More than making up for my last post outside in the cold, here I caught my best assignment during the entire detail. I was posted on stage at the podium to maintain security until the arrival of President Reagan and his detail.

For probably the only time as I recall, the President was late getting to the event. While we were waiting, I had a chance to chat with Art Fleming (*Jeopardy* host) who was the emcee for the event. After learning I was from Raleigh, he said that he had once worked at a radio station in nearby Rocky Mount.

As time passed the crowd was getting a little restless, so one of the campaign officials suggested that they ask Bob Hope (who was there for the rally) to come on stage to entertain the folks until the President arrived. He reportedly sent word back that he was not an opening act for anyone. True or not I do not know, but he did not come on stage until President Reagan arrived.

On November 4th, we flew to Los Angeles for Presidential campaign visits and the expected victory party on election night at the Century Plaza Hotel where the President stayed. He, of course, won reelection carrying all states but Minnesota, the home state of Mr. Mondale. The election night event at the Century Plaza was rather exciting and enjoyable. With rotating post assignments, you got a chance to see what was going on pretty much throughout the evening. On an outside post at the entrance to the underground garage, I got to meet and speak briefly with Chuck Connors (*The Rifleman*). While on a crowd surveillance posts inside the hotel, you had an opportunity to see many politicians and Hollywood types.

With the election over, we were released from our details and I returned to Raleigh. Part of me was glad it was over, but another part wanted to continue for just another week or so. I would not want to do it permanently, but for those few months it was exciting and enjoyable. I would never have had the chance to go to the places we went to, stay in the hotels we stayed in, or seen the people I saw.

At the outset as noted above, I had heard stories of how non-Secret Service agents were treated poorly including given all the bad posts, poor lodging, and being referred to as a "OTA'. I did not find that to be the case at all on my detail. Our lodging arrangements (Grand Hyatt, Beverly Hilton) were the same as theirs, our post assignments were fairly assigned (some good and some not so good), and as to the OTA reference some felt demeaning, I was never referred to as such and only saw it written on the first assignment sheet.

Chapter Sixteen
FIREARMS AND ARSON CASES (1984-1985)

924(c) Cases

In the early 1980s, ATF became much more active in the "War on Drugs" through the federal firearms laws. Section 924(c) of the GCA of 1968, carrying/using a firearm during a drug trafficking crime became the primary ATF violation charged. During the same period, the North Carolina prisons became over-crowded, resulting in prisoners being released early, sometime after serving only one-fourth of their sentence.

As a result, local and state officers turned to ATF and the federal courts, knowing federal convictions resulted in longer prison sentence. Section 924(c), for example, carried a mandatory five-year sentence for the first offense and twenty years for second and subsequent offenses.

Under the Armed Career Criminal Enhancement Act 924(e), felons in possession of firearms with three prior convictions for serious drug offenses and/or violent felonies carried a mandatory 15-year sentence. And under the federal system, five years meant five years and fifteen years meant fifteen years with very little time reduction possible for good behavior. We tried to take as many of the referrals as possible, which resulted in ATF and the federal courts being overwhelmed with the "adopted cases".

Unlicensed Dealer Cases

One of the most difficult to prove and seldom charged violation of the GCA of 1968, was dealing in firearms without a license. Section 923(a) states that no person shall engage in the business of dealing in firearms until he has filed an application and received a license, and Section 922 (a) says that it is unlawful for any person, other than a licensee, to engage in the business of dealing in firearms.

The phrase "engage in the business" was not defined and open to a lot of interpretations. Initially, if an individual sold a firearm on three separate occasions, he could be considered engaged in the business. With that definition, a large number of people, including several police officers, would be considered in the business requiring a federal firearms license. Through administrative rulings and court decisions, that definition was determined to be too broad and insufficient to define and establish "engaging in the business".

As time passed, the term "engaged in the business" came to mean a person truly in the business of buying and selling firearms on a continuous basis, as a livelihood and for a profit. I liken it to a Supreme Court pornography case wherein one of the Justices said "it (pornography) is hard to define but you know it when you see it."

One of the few unlicensed dealer cases at the Raleigh office occurred in 1989, when information was received that a man was selling stolen guns in Wake County. Through an informant, the man was identified as Paul E. An investigation was opened and Special Agent Ron Tunkel, in an undercover capacity, contacted Paul E. about buying some guns.

Over a three- month period, Tunkel met with Paul E. several times and purchased a total of fifteen pistols, primarily cheap Saturday Night Specials. During the undercover contacts, Paul E. confided to Tunkel that he had been buying and selling guns for ten to fifteen years; that he got most of his guns from a pawn shop in Rome, Georgia; and sold most of them in Tennessee and North Carolina. He told Tunkel he usually made about $25 profit per gun, but on a couple occasions he was able to get stolen guns and turn them over for a bigger profit. We arrested Paul E. in Raleigh when he made the final delivery of four Raven .25 caliber semiautomatic pistols. He was convicted in federal court for violations of the federal firearms laws, including dealing in firearms without a license.

Ross Investigation

In December 1984, Texas State Troopers stopped and searched a car on I-10 near El Paso, that resulted in the discovery and seizure of six Ruger Mini-14 rifles, two 12-gauge shotguns, 2,000 rounds of .223 ammunition, and fifty shotgun shells. The driver of the vehicle, Jerson Martinez, stated that he had been hired to pick up the guns in North Carolina and bring them to Texas. Examination of the rifles revealed that they had been converted to fire fully automatics. The rifles were traced to Thomerson's Gun Shop in Creedmoor, North Carolina.

Subsequent investigation and surveillance revealed that former Major Violator Doug Ross (Chapter 4) had contacted Thomerson and asked him to convert the rifles to fully automatic to trade for drugs with Mexican drug dealers. Thomerson converted fourteen mini-14 rifles to fully automatic and delivered them to Ross on two separate occasions, once in Asheville and once in Newport, Tennessee. Ross paid Thomerson $1,000 for each rifle. An ATF case was submitted to the US Attorney's Office, charging Ross and his associates with multiple violations of the Federal Firearms laws.

During the same period, Ross, identified as a major drug trafficker, was the target of a FBI, IRS, SBI, and Durham Police organized crime task force investigation in Durham. Their investigation led to a federal indictment charging Ross and his associates with drug trafficking. But when it came arrest time, Ross was nowhere to be found. He had gotten wind of the indictments and fled.

Although we (ATF) were not active participants in the FBI investigation, we and they were aware of the parallel investigations and shared some information. After the indictment of Ross, FBI agent Jim Roche and I joined in our efforts to locate him. Based on Ross's past history and information from informants, we knew that Ross trusted very few and when he felt the need to lay low, he would go to the mountains to some of his old bootlegging buddies who he felt he could trust.

We spent several weeks looking for him in and around Asheville, Wilkes County and eastern Tennessee with no results. Having found no trace of him, I contacted several old liquor informants, one of whom told me that Doug had gone to Florida to buy drugs. He said that Ross had become addicted to cocaine and alcohol, and was pretty much under the influence all the time, often to the point of having to have someone drive for him. He further stated that Ross and his driver had left with about $300K to go to Florida to purchase cocaine and would be back in about a week.

The informant speculated that when Ross did not return after several weeks that something had happened to him in Florida. Although the informant had been proven reliable in the past, both Roche and I were a little skeptical thinking the Florida story might had been concocted so that we would stop looking for him. We continued searching for Doug but never located him.

A Task Force agent later informed me that Ross and an associate had been murdered in Florida. He said that one of Ross's oldest and trusted liquor associates, who was dying of cancer, had come forward to say that he had killed Ross. He related how he was in Miami, in dire need of money, and had called Doug and told him he had a large quantity of cocaine he needed to sell. That Doug and one of his associates had driven down with $300k to buy the cocaine; that he shot both of them, took the money, and covered up their bodies. The bodies were subsequently found and identified through dental records to be Doug Ross and an associate from Burlington, North Carolina. Doug Ross, a major liquor violator and drug trafficker who I had come to know at the outset of my career and occasionally throughout, was now dead. Or was he?

Several years after I retired, I was at a junkyard in Granville County looking for a tailgate for an old truck I had bought and struck up a conversation with the owner. As we talked, the subject of Doug Ross came up and I related the information I had received about Doug's death. He laughed and said, "Man that is a bunch of bullshit. Doug Ross is not dead. Hell, I have seen him myself several times after the time you say he was killed."

He went on to say that Doug had saved up millions of dollars and that the Miami story was just to get you all off his back. To him and many others in Franklin and Granville counties, Doug was admired and looked up to — a cross between Al Capone and Robin Hood. I thought about re-contacting the agent who had told me the story and to try to document and verify that Doug Ross was indeed dead as reported. But after thinking about it, I decided not to because I, too, had a degree of admiration and respect for Doug. So, let the legend and the man perhaps live on.

Doug's (or whoever's) remains were returned from Florida and now rest in the family cemetery at Mary's Chapel Baptist Church in Grissom, North Carolina.

The Meanest Man in Wake County

In December, the Zebulon Police Department requested ATF assistance in a firearms investigation relative to James Adams, a convicted felon described as the most significant criminal in their area. Adams's car had been found at the scene of an attempted burglary, and during the search of the car they found a loaded pistol. Adams's fingerprints were found in the car and on the pistol. The pistol was traced to a local resident, who admitted giving the gun to Adams. Investigation revealed that Adams was a very violent felon with numerous assault charges. One of the convictions was for assaulting Wake County officers trying to break up a fight at a local bar. A number of the officers were injured, and one officer sustained permanent impairment as a result of the vicious assault by Adams and his cohorts.

Adams was indicted and arrested for possession of a firearm by a convicted felon. Given his record and reputation of violence and intimidation of witnesses, we asked that he be detained until his trial. Under the Bail Reform Act of 1984, defendants could be held in custody and denied bail if they were considered a flight risk or a danger to the public. We brought in several local officers to testify as to his character, reputation, and history of violence, one of which described him as the "meanest man in Wake and surrounding counties." The Judge found him to be a danger to the public and possible witnesses in the case, and ordered him held in custody until his trial. Several months later he was convicted and sent to federal prison. At sentencing the Judge reviewed and commented on his lengthy record after which Adams's attorney pointed out to the Judge that there had been nothing at all on his record over the past nine months. The Judge suggested to the attorney that perhaps that could be explained by the fact that he had been in jail the past nine months.

Several years after I retired, Raleigh agent Ken Andrews contacted me about the Adams case. He told me that they had again charged Adams with violations of the federal firearms laws including possession of a firearm by a convicted felon. To establish that he was indeed a convicted felon, Andrews asked me to testify regarding his previous conviction in federal court in my case back in 1985. I testified as to his previous conviction, and he was found guilty and again sentenced to federal prison. I think I read or heard some time later that he had died of cancer.

Sparkles Nightclub Fire Investigation

Shortly after midnight on February 20, 1985, the Raleigh Fire Department responded to a fire at the Sparkles Nightclub on Hodges Street, which resulted in the destruction of the building and its contents. Subsequent fire scene investigation by the Raleigh Fire and Police personnel resulted in the conclusion that the fire was intentionally set. They determined that the business was owned by Walid S. and Ramzi R. Both were interviewed along with manager Bill L., and all said the business was doing well and they had no knowledge as to how the fire might have started. The owners subsequently filed a claim with his insurance company for loses totaling $450,000.

Approximately one year later, the insurance adjuster contacted ATF and requested an investigation be conducted relative to the fire and reported losses. Special Agent Ed Garrison and I were assigned to look into the matter. After examining police and fire reports, the evidence gathered by them, and talking with the officers involved, it appeared to be little doubt that the fire was intentionally set. As to who and why, the first thing you always look at in these type cases is who had a motive and stood to gain from the fire. Given the $450,000 insurance claim, the obvious suspects would be the owners and the collection of the insurance money the motive. During their statements to the police and the insurance company, Walid S., Ramzi R., and Bill L. all claimed that the business was profitable. They said they were making enough to pay the bills with money left over. Ed and I also interviewed the three, and each again stated that the business was good, and they were making money.

However, as we began to contact suppliers and vendors as well as the owner of the building, a different picture as to the health and prosperity of the business emerged. They were behind in their lease payments to the building owner to the point that they had been notified that litigation was being initiated to collect the $11,000 owed. They were behind in equipment lease payments to the point the leasing company was initiating action to re-possess the equipment. They had been notified by the NC ABC Board that due to violations that their ABC permits/licenses were going to be suspended or revoked. (An ABC hearing date on the revocation was set for February 25th, five day after the fire.)

We subpoenaed all business and financial records associated with the business, which were examined and analyzed by an ATF Auditor. He found that the business was debt ridden and insolvent at the time of the fire, that for the nine-month period prior to the fire the business actually lost $82,000, and that the money invested in the business was grossly overstated and that losses reported to the insurance company were grossly overstated.

In this case, as in most arson for profit cases, fraudulent policy claims and supporting documents were sent to the insurance company through the US Postal Service, thereby constituting a mail fraud violation, which could be proven. As the investigation continued, it became pretty clear that Walid S. and Ramzi R. were behind the fire for the insurance money, and that they paid Bill L. to actually set the fire. We felt that we had a case for conspiracy and arson violations, but perhaps a little more was needed. Bill L. had made several contradicting statements in various statements to police and fire investigators, the insurance company, and to us during our interviews.

Assistant US Attorney (AUSA) Kieran Shanahan, who had been assisting in the investigation with Grand Jury subpoenas, suggested that Bill L. be subpoenaed to testify before the Federal Grand Jury. Shanahan and later Assistant United States Attorney Bill Webb were somewhat of a new breed in the US Attorney Office. They were aggressive, enforcement minded, and eager to get involved during the investigative stage of a case. Heretofore, as a matter of routine the agent conducted his investigation, made his case and then the AUSA assigned would take over and direct the prosecution of the case. This worked well in liquor and most firearms investigations, but in the case of complex bombing and arson cases it was essential to have an active, competent, aggressive AUSA involved in the investigation almost from the outset. And if you looked in Mr. Webster's dictionary for the attributes of such an individual, you might see brilliant, skillful, well-spoken, assertive, forceful, gutsy, fierce, unyielding, competitive, bold, self-assured and more. Or a picture of Mr. Shanahan would more than suffice.

Bill L. was subpoenaed and did appear, repeating his previously contradicting statements, some of which we had evidence to prove were untrue. So, he was indicted for lying to the federal grand jury and after a short time in the US Marshall's lockup decided to come clean and cooperate. He admitted the business was going broke and about to lose their liquor/beer license, and that Walid S, and Ramzi R, offered him $10,000 to burn the building, which he did. He agreed to wear a wire and meet with the two owners to discuss setting the fire.

All three were subsequently arrested, convicted in Federal court, and sentenced to federal prison. They were represented by a former Congressman and also Raleigh attorney Wade Smith, I believe, who pled for short sentences. Judge Dupree was, I thought, relatively lenient in his sentencing and surprisingly did not cut Bill L. any slack for his cooperation.

Goldsboro Arson Ring

In May 1985, SBI Agent Phil Brinkley and Wayne County Sheriff Detective Larry Pierce received information from an informant that there was a group in Wayne County setting fires for money. SBI Agent Brinkley contacted ATF and requested that Agent Garrison and I assist in the investigation. Through the informant it was learned that Greg was the ringleader, and the actual torches were identified to be Todd and Mike. An undercover sting investigation was initiated wherein ATF Agent Roger Brown, in an undercover role, hired the three to burn a building he owned. As the investigation proceeded, we found it difficult to actually find a building to suit our needs. A couple of possibilities failed though when the owners had second thoughts that the building might indeed burn. One building found was a car wash in Durham, but that just didn't sound right "burn a car wash"

Through Charlotte ATF Agent Jim Roberts and Charlotte Arson Task Force officer Terry Lacey, we were able to locate a restaurant in Charlotte that was closed and up for sale. It fit the undercover story that the undercover agent had a business that he had been trying to sell. The deal was set, and the initial payment was made. The plan was that Todd and Mike would attend a concert in Greensboro with friends and would slip out early and drive to Charlotte and torch the building around midnight.

On that night we had the building surrounded, and four of us were actually inside the building to take them down when they entered. Shortly after midnight their car was spotted in the area, they then parked and walked to the building carrying a jug of gasoline. Inside we could hear them as they walked up to the door, and then nothing for a few seconds. The outside agents informed us that they just walked back to the car and left leaving behind the jug of gasoline.

Through subsequent undercover contact we learned that they had seen a police car drive by and thought they heard something in the building. They decided things just were not right and according to one "something told me to not go in the building". They agreed to come back later and finish the job, but not having control of when that might be, we decided to go ahead and make the arrest and charge them with conspiracy as well as the attempted arson.

Prior to trial, their attorneys filed an entrapment defense, claiming that they were entrapped by the government. Entrapment occurs when government agents persuade or entice someone to commit a criminal act that they would not otherwise do. To overcome that defense, the government must demonstrate that they were already prone to do that and in fact were in the business (burning building for money in this case). When a defendant pleads entrapment, he, in effect, admits he did the criminal act and so when the judge ruled against their entrapment defense, they pled guilty and were sentenced.

United Nations Detail

In October 1985, ATF agents were assigned to assist the Secret Service at the United Nations General Assembly in New York. The U.N. was celebrating its 40th anniversary, and heads of states and dignitaries from all over the world were attending. Special Agents Devaney, McAleer and I were assigned from the Raleigh office. I was on a security detail for Abballah Abderemane, the President of Comoros. Devaney and McAleer were on a protective detail for Desire Bouterse, the Chief of State of Suriname.

217

Quite honestly, I had never heard of either man or his country. My detail was pretty easy and boring, as Mr. Abderemane always returned to his hotel room and stayed in after leaving the daily UN activities. Some of the heads of states and dignitaries were a little more active, which required agents to work a little harder. One head of state wanted to see Disneyland and, of course, his security detail had to travel with him there.

Chapter Seventeen
TASK FORCE CASES (1986-1989)

S AC John Westra and ASAC Steve Whitlow retired in 1985, bringing about a new leadership team in the Charlotte District. Dave Conklin was named the new SAC and Chuck Stanfill was named the new ASAC. Mr. Conklin served as SAC for only a few months and left for some type of personal reason, as I recall. He was a very likeable guy and seemed to be a real straight shooter. Paul Lyon was named the new SAC and ushered in the Lyon-Stanfill regime, which lasted ten years—the same amount of time as their predecessors. In 1988, Phil McGuire retired, and Dan Hartnett succeeded him as the Associate Director Law Enforcement (ADLE).

Agent Don Devaney retired in 1987, and two new agents, Ron Tunkel and Bill Marshall were assigned to the Raleigh office. Both turned out to be outstanding agents and had very successful careers. Ron became an ATF Profiler stationed at Quantico, Virginia at the FBI facility. Bill became a Certified Fire Investigator working primarily with the ATF National Response Team. Two years later just prior to my departure, new agents Jaime Colley, Ken Andrews, Michael Fanelly, and Harold McCluney were assigned to the Raleigh office

Dale Winters
On Thursday night June 26, 1986, former ATF Special Agent Dale Winters laid down on his bed in cell #S-4 at the Mecklenburg County Jail in Charlotte less than two days after being convicted of firebombing his estranged wife's apartment. Sometime during the night as he laid face down on the bed, he pulled a plastic garbage bag over his head, sealed the open end with a rubber band around his neck and held the bag tightly with his hands until he lost conscious and died. What had happened in the short eight years since

he was sworn in as a new Special Agent and reported to the ATF office in Charlotte?

Dale reported to the Charlotte office in the spring of 1978 after a brief stint as a police officer in Florida. Prior to that he had served in the army as a helicopter pilot in Vietnam, where he was decorated for valor and courageous service. I recall Dale as being soft spoken, a bit shy, and maybe a little naïve—none of which fit the "war hero" image. He fit in well with everyone and appeared to have a very bright future with ATF.

There was some talk of Dale and his wife having some marital issues. The best I remember, she was not totally happy with his job and them living in Charlotte. I left as the Charlotte supervisor and returned to Raleigh shortly after he came aboard. After that, I would see Dale occasionally at statewide meetings and from everything I heard, he learned and progressed quickly and had become a real go-getter investigator. As time passed, I heard he had transferred to Miami, but had no understanding as to the "what and whys" behind the move.

And then came the news that he had been arrested for attempting to firebomb his wife's apartment in Charlotte. It was like something you hear and say, "No way! This can't be true!" But it was! The stories going around were that he and his wife had separated, and he had gotten involved with some women in Miami. It was said that Dale had gotten to "running with a fast crowd" including drug users, and had gotten in way over his head. Though there was that bit of naivety, I just can't understand how things could have gone so wrong for Dale. I can only imagine the depth of shame, hopelessness, and despair that he faced on that June night. Tears come to my eyes every time I think about that night and what it must have been like for Dale and his conclusion that death was the only way out.

Hells Angels

In January 1986, a San Francisco Drug Task Force investigation was opened regarding violations of the federal firearms, explosives, and narcotics laws by the Hells Angel Motorcycle Club (HAMC). The investigation was opened when Tony Tait, an officer in the Anchorage HAMC, agreed to become a confidential informant and work for the FBI and ATF. Anchorage FBI agent Ken Marischen and San Francisco ATF agent Ted Baltas controlled the CI and directed the overall investigation. In August, an Anchorage HAMC member was shot and killed in Louisville, Kentucky by two members of the rival Outlaw Motorcycle Club (OMC). The murder rekindled a long-standing feud between the two clubs. The HAMC planned to retaliate against the OMC and Tait, a charter and national HAMC officer highly trusted within the organization, was given the responsibility of obtaining explosives and weapons for the retaliation. Tait visited HAMC chapters throughout the country and was able to purchase narcotics, firearms, and explosives.

In February 1987, Tait attended the HAMC East Coast Officers Meeting in Charleston, South Carolina, during which he met and talked with Lawrence Dean Lenihan (aka Chitlin), the president of the Durham HAMC chapter. In discussing the upcoming retaliation against the OMC, Lenihan said the Durham chapter had some C-4 (a military high explosives) and a LAW rocket (Military light Anti-tank Weapon). In subsequent meetings, Lenihan and Timothy Blackwell (aka Tiny), Durham chapter Treasurer, told Tait they would furnish five lbs. of C-4 and some blasting caps. In April, Blackwell and fellow club member Larry White delivered five lbs. of C-4 and eight Dupont electric blasting caps to Tait at the Radisson Hotel in Durham. They suggested to Tait that he should use two of the caps to set off the C-4.

In November, search warrants were executed, and arrests were made at several HAMC Chapter locations throughout the country. Locally, Lenihan was arrested at the clubhouse and Blackwell and White were arrested at their residences. Sixteen members across the country including Sonny Barger, president of the Oakland chapter and recognized head of the HAMC nationally, were indicted and tried for conspiracy and violations of the federal explosives laws in Louisville, Kentucky. Lenihan, Blackwell and White were severed from the Louisville trial and remanded for trial in the Middle Judicial District of NC. The conspiracy trial in Louisville lasted three months and turned out to be somewhat of a fiasco. Barger and one other defendant were found guilty of conspiracy, but the remaining defendants were found not guilty of the major charges.

In September 1990, Lenihan, Blackwell, and White were tried in US Middle District Court in Greensboro. They, of course, were represented by high-priced lawyers, and given the fiasco in Louisville I did have some concerns about the outcome. My concerns were (1) the trial might be a repeat of the Louisville trial, which was chaotic and sometimes more a circus atmosphere rather than federal court trial; (2) I had some doubt as to whether the Assistant US Attorney handling the case was experienced and tough enough; (3) that the jury might be intimidated by not only three HAMC on trial but also the presence of members in the audience each day; and, (4) that the jury would not understand that the C-4 and blasting caps with intent constituted an explosives device which constituted a federal firearms violation. My misgivings were for naught as the jury found all three guilty and they were sentenced to federal prison. The judge maintained order and decorum throughout the trial and the AUSA did a very good job. As to the jury not understanding the firearms violation, ATF Explosives Expert Jerry Taylor's and ATF Chemist Lloyd Erwin's testimony tied everything together, and the jury was obviously not intimidated.

Raleigh Jamaicans (Rjam)

In the mid-1980s, law enforcement in the US became aware that Jamaican Posses (gangs) were importing and selling large quantities of narcotics in the US. The Jamaican posse members were largely convicted felons and/or illegal aliens who had migrated from Jamaican to the US. Unlike some other cartels who bring in large bulk quantities, then sell in bulk to middlemen, who then sell to distributers, the Jamaicans take care of it all. Some members import, some are wholesalers, and some are street level distributors. By cutting out the middlemen and handling the entire operation from import to street sales, their profit margins were higher.

They were also very violent and responsible for an estimated 600 drug-related homicides during the mid-1980s, a large number unsolved due to the fact that many victims are illegal aliens with no identification. Law enforcement also found it difficult to get a handle on the Jamaicans, as most used fictitious names and addresses, often just going by "street names". They also found them to be tightly organized and mobile, making it extremely difficult to get informants and/or undercover officer in the organizations. Their MO was to set up in a large city like New York or Miami, and then send out members to smaller cities to set up and operate the drug distribution. If they committed a violent crime or homicide or were about to be arrested, they would simply flee, and others would be sent to take their place.

ATF initially got involved with the Jamaican Posse by tracing firearms used by them in narcotics, homicide, and other violent crimes. It was learned that the Jamaicans obtained firearms by straw purchases, thefts and robberies, and falsification of firearms dealers' records. In an investigation in Tampa, Florida, two Jamaicans were arrested, and sixty-seven firearms and several boxes of ammunition were seized. Subsequent investigation revealed that the two Jamaicans had purchased 149 firearms from various dealers in the Tampa area. It was determined that once purchased, the guns were delivered to high-ranking members for distribution to the street members.

In early 1987, the Raleigh Police Department began receiving information relative to drug trafficking by Jamaican Nationals. They started making arrests and seizures of narcotics, usually in small amounts of marijuana, cocaine, and crack. They discovered that the Jamaicans were very violent and, in most cases, carried and/ or used firearms in their drug trafficking activities. They quickly realized that given their local jurisdiction, they needed additional expertise and resources. In February 1988, an Organized Crime Drug Task Force (OCDETF) investigation was initiated with the Raleigh Police Department, the NC State Bureau of Investigation, Wake County Sheriff's Department, DEA, Immigration and Naturalization Service and ATF participating. The stated objective was that working in close liaison with the Wake County District Attorney Office and the United States Attorney's office, to successfully identify, arrest and prosecute those involved in the narcotics distribution and criminal possession and use of firearms.

The Raleigh Jamaican Task Force (Rjam) operated out of the Raleigh Police Department, and while I don't recall that if we had an official designated leader, Sergeant Mike Longmire ran the day-to-day operations. Raleigh PD had nine officers assigned, the SBI three, and one each from the Wake County Sheriff's Office, DEA, INS, and ATF. Assistant United States Attorney Bill Webb was the primary representative from the US Attorney's office.

Somewhat surprisingly to me, everyone seemed to get along and the task force concept functioned pretty well. Going in I was aware of some distrust, animosities, and conflicts among some of the participating agencies. The Raleigh PD and the Wake County Sheriff's Department did not get along at all and seldom worked together. That feeling was nurtured and enforced from the very top, I was told. Both departments had the reputation as being overly independent and handled everything on their own. Both were very distrustful of outside agencies and officers, especially from the federal side. They felt (and rightly so in some cases) that when working with the Feds it was always a one-way road. The feds would take, but never give. Personally, I had worked with officers from both departments, more so with Raleigh officers, and never had any problems at all.

Despite my reservations, real or perceived, the task force continued to function for almost two years with few problems. In looking back, I think the task force functioned as smoothly as it did for a couple reasons. First of all, the people assigned got along well and we even had some fun along the way. And secondly, I think everyone realized that they (their agency) could not do it alone; that everyone brought something to the table. Raleigh PD had the personnel and officers on the street gathering information and intelligence on the gangs, the SBI had computer expertise and intelligence data, ATF and DEA had the federal violations and access to the federal courts, and most important was the INS whose expertise in identifying the suspects and their citizenship status proved invaluable.

When the investigation was closed, 315 criminal charges (federal and state) had been made against 156 individuals. Twenty-one were federal defendants, fifteen of whom had pled guilty, two were awaiting trial and four were fugitives. Thirty-three additional suspects were waiting indictment and trial, twenty-eight of which were identified as deportable Jamaican aliens. Thirty-two firearms and drugs valued in excess of $500,000 were seized along with forfeitable assets in excess of $550,000. Most importantly, the Jamaicans decided that Raleigh was not a good place to do business and they left.

Pig – Two

On the night of April 13, 1987, a fire occurred at the Piggly Wiggly grocery store at Fuquay-Varina, North Carolina, resulting in extensive damage to the building and contents. A cause and origin investigation conducted by the Charlotte ATF Response Team and the North Carolina State Bureau of Investigation determined that there were three separate points of origin. The owner, Harry T., maintained that the store was doing well and was profitable. Subsequent investigation by the Raleigh ATF, North Carolina SBI, and the United States Attorney's Office revealed that the store was not profitable at all and in dire financial shape. It revealed that Harry T. had diverted money from the business to himself, had tried to sell the business, and was in the process of filing for bankruptcy. It was also determined that Harry T. was seen by police near the store at the time of the fire. In statements to ATF case agent Bill Marshall and others, Harry T. continually made misleading and false statements relative to the fire and attempted to divert suspicion to others.

Harry T. was eventually indicted by a federal Grand Jury and after a three-week trial was convicted of arson, mail fraud, and making a false statement. He was sentenced to twenty-four months in prison and five years of probation. He was also ordered to make restitution in the amount of $125,000 to the insurance company.

And yes, there was a Pig-One. In that case, a Piggly Wiggly grocery store in Chadbourn, North Carolina was destroyed by a fire in 1982. One of the first "arson for profit" cases in the Division, the investigation was led by Wilmington ATF Agent Charlie Mercer. His investigation revealed that the fire was intentionally set to destroy the building and contents to collect the insurance. The owners were charged and convicted in federal court.

Note: Piggly Wiggly is a grocery store chain operating primarily in the Southeast and Midwest regions of the US. It is the oldest grocery chain in the country, having been started in Memphis, Tennessee in 1916. Like all Piggly Wiggly stores, the Fuquay-Varina and Chadbourn stores were franchises and independently owned and operated.

Liberty Warehouse

In the mid-'80s, as Americans became more aware of the health hazards of smoking, the sale and consumption of cigarettes started to decline significantly. The tobacco industry, feeling the change, started to adjust to the changing market. Manufacturers consolidated, and in a lot of cases just shut down operations. The large tobacco warehouses that had been for decades the place where farmers brought their crop for sale were no longer a necessary part of the process. So, owners were left with these empty large tobacco warehouses. Some were converted for other uses like flea markets and storage facilities, and some mysteriously caught fire and burned to the ground. One such was the Liberty Warehouse in Wilson, which was destroyed by fire in the spring of 1987.

Investigation conducted by ATF, SBI, and local agents revealed that the fire had been intentionally set and that the owners had paid a professional arsonist to burn the building and its contents to collect the insurance. Information revealed that the arson ring was headed by an individual known as Harvey, who operated in Ayden, North Carolina. According to sources, Harvey was basically a "crime broker" who could arrange (for a fee) any type of criminal activity one might need, such as the burning of a building. After undercover attempts and other traditional investigative efforts failed to get to Harvey, it was decided that a Title III wiretap would probably be the only way to obtain evidence against Harvey. ATF case agent Dave Lazar and Assistant US Attorney Shanahan put together the request, and a Federal Court Order was obtained to tap his telephone and install transmitters in his office.

At that time, Title III wiretaps were not something ATF did every day and, quite honestly, not fully prepared to carry out. It was certainly the only one I was ever involved in during my career. The ATF technicians who came down from Headquarters to plant the transmitters had some issues getting into the building and installing the devices. We quickly discovered that the listening and monitoring would require a lot of manpower.

ATF and SBI agents across the state were brought in to help with the monitoring at great expense for lodging, per diem and scheduled overtime. We were obtaining some valuable information, but nothing really related to the arson.

After a number of weeks, Lazar and AUSA Shanahan made the decision to shut down the operation. A case report was prepared, charging the two owners of the warehouse, the arsonist, and Harvey with arson and conspiracy. The torch and the two owners, a father and son, were tried in Federal court. The torch and son were convicted but the father was found not guilty. Harvey died of a heart attack before the court proceedings.

Chapter Eighteen
MOONSHINE TO MANAGEMENT – TAKE TWO (1990-1994)

W ith the Raleigh Jamaican, Hells Angels, and cigarette smuggling investigations coming to a close, things started to settle down a little for me. I still had a minimum of four years and a maximum of eleven years to go before retirement, and I was not sure what I wanted to do. I knew I didn't want to spend the rest of my career— as one agent put it—"chasing young punk drug dealers with guns through the streets of Raleigh and Durham".

By the time you get to my stage in your career, you need to have found a specialization or niche. Ed Garrison had found his as Certified Fire Investigator (CFI) and David McAleer had found his expertise in firearms. My expertise and niche had been in moonshining, gambling, and cigarettes, but when they all fizzled out, so did my niche. So, I thought maybe another try in management might be in order. After all, I was certainly more mature, experienced, and knowledgeable than I was in 1977. It so happened that three RAC jobs were coming open in the Division: Wilmington, Fayetteville, and Winston-Salem. The pay grade was the same GS-13, but there was talk that the RAC position was going to be upgraded to a GS-14. After making a little inquiry, I found out that Wilmington and Fayetteville were spoken for, but that I might have a chance for the Winston-Salem position. I applied and was selected.

I reported to Winston-Salem in May 1990. The office, in the federal building downtown, was rather small with an office for the RAC, a reception area, two small storage rooms, and one large squad room for all the agents. Janet Glascoe was the secretary, and the agents were Ernie Driver, Allan Melton, Larry Morrissey, Chris Olson, Kenny Spann, Ted Warren, Doug Wenner, and Deborah West. Agents Morrissey and Wenner were the only two veteran agents, having transferred into the division from Pittsburg and

Boston. Agent Warren had been with ATF for about three years, coming on board from the Durham Police Department, and the others had been on less than two years. Agent Driver had come over from the NC SBI; Melton from the SC Highway Patrol; Olson from the Lancaster, SC Sheriff's Department; Spann from the Charlotte Police Department; and West from the NC Highway Patrol. Although new to ATF, the younger agents were all experienced officers with law enforcement backgrounds.

The office was dealing with a recent shooting incident, wherein Agent Warren had shot a violator during the execution of a search warrant. Otherwise, things appeared to be going pretty smoothly. Everyone seemed to be getting along well, and the agents were making cases. As a result of his years of experience with the Durham PD, Ted Warren was the hard-charger, big-case guy and looked up to by the others in the office. Working with IRS agent Ted Warren (that's right two Ted Warrens: Gun-Ted and Money-Ted), officers of the Winston-Salem PD and Assistant United States Attorney Paul Weinman, Warren was conducting a major drug/firearms investigation in Winston-Salem. The investigation resulted in arrests and convictions for drug and firearms violation and the seizure of $600,000 cash. Agent Warren also developed a CI within the Winston-Salem chapter of the Hells Angels Motorcycle, and as result made a drug/firearms case against members of the HAMC.

In June, I sent a request for additional office space to the SAC. He agreed that we needed more space, and informed me that he had wanted to relocate the office to Greensboro (be careful what you ask for). He directed me to draft a proposal and justification for the relocation. The proposal was submitted in July and approved by ATF Headquarters in September.

After the approval, we started the initial process through GSA to locate a suitable building, configure the office space to include a vault for seized property, telephones, alarms, and all the other many things needed. To put it mildly, it turned out to be a very lengthy, challenging, and often frustrating process trying to deal with the GSA and other related people. They move at their pace—not yours. The relocation was approved in September 1990, and we remained in Winston-Salem until July 1993 when we finally moved into our new office in Greensboro.

If given a choice, I think most of the agents had rather we stayed in Winston-Salem, since most lived west of Winston-Salem. Janet was very apprehensive about the move and as much as we I tried to persuade her to make the move, she made the decision to transfer back to the Veterans Administration and remain in Winston-Salem where all her friends were. We conducted interviews and hired Barbara Osborne to replace Janet as the secretary. Interestingly, Barbara later got an Inspector position and Janet returned as the Secretary in Greensboro. It was really a win-win outcome for everyone.

A few months after arriving at the POD, I started to hear some rumblings about Agent West not wanting to go on searches, arrests, etc. I called her into my office, at which time she told me that she was unhappy with the job and uncomfortable with some of the things she was told she had to do. She said no one ever told her that she would have to go on searches, make arrests, deal with informers, and be exposed to the unpleasantness and danger of dealing with the criminals.

I explained to her that that was we (ATF) did; that we conducted investigations and made cases against criminals, often unpleasant and violent people; and that conducting searches, making arrests, dealing with informants and criminals, and working odd and long hours were a necessary and crucial part of the job. As we talked, I recalled that she had been a local officer and a trooper with the NC State Highway Patrol and certainly should have had some idea what ATF agents and law enforcement officers in general did.

After several conversations about the matter, it became obvious that she did not want to and probably could not do the things that the job required. I suggested to her that she might need to start looking for another job, and she agreed that would be the thing to do. A few weeks later, she informed me that she had applied for a job with the State, in the Revenue Department as an agent doing civil asset seizures and forfeitures in connection with criminal drug arrests and seizures.

In keeping with expectations and policy, I informed the ASAC and SAC of the situation and the fact she would be leaving shortly. The SAC cautioned me to be very careful in handling the matter, pointing out that it was a delicate situation her being a female agent and what she might say about her leaving. I was well aware that any allegations made by a female or black male toward a white male superior, whether true or not, would bring down the wrath of hell upon that supervisor. There would be internal affairs, EEO, Justice Department, *Sixty Minutes*, and probably others conducting investigations to set the wrong right. I tried to assure the SAC (and perhaps myself) that Agent West was not going to make any allegations of mistreatment or wrongdoing, and that she was resigning as soon as she got the job with the State.

She got the job with the State a short time later and left, to my knowledge, with no hard feelings. Several of the agents and I had contact with her later, and she stated that she was really happy with her new job. Unfortunately, the position was eliminated as a result of a court decision that the civil assessments and penalties, in addition to the criminal penalties, created a double jeopardy. I think by that time she had married an officer with the Chatham County Sheriff's Department and started a family. I last saw her in Pittsboro in a police uniform directing traffic and spoke with her briefly. I don't know if she was an officer with the department or just an auxiliary member helping out with a fire emergency. A few years later, I learned that she had died of cancer—so sad at such an early age with two young children.

On the night of September 13, 1990, shortly before midnight, my residence telephone rung and I answered it. "Johnny, this is Ted," are the exact words I heard, followed by, "Ernie and I were involved in a shooting incident in Ashe County." After determining that neither he nor Ernie (or other officers) were hurt, and neither of them did the shooting, I was able to breathe again. He continued on to tell me what had happened. He said that he and Ernie had been contacted by officers of the High South Interstate Drug Task Force (a drug task force made up of officers from Ashe, Avery and Watauga counties) to assist in a buy/bust of Glen D., an armed drug dealer in Boone. After two undercover purchases of cocaine from Glen D., Officer Bob Kennedy of the Boone Police had made arrangements with Glen D. to trade stolen property for cocaine. The buy/bust was to take place in a motel in Boone, with cover teams assigned for the take down. Warren and Driver were assigned to one of the cover teams.

As the plans were being made, Glen D. contacted Kennedy and changed the meeting place to "a white house" in rural Ashe County. The take down plans were changed and the teams were re-positioned near "the white house'. The plan called for Kennedy to say the code words, "It's a done deal," at which time the two cover teams would converge to assist in the arrest. But at the very last minute, Glen D. told Kennedy to back down a dirt road (behind "the white house") to a small stream, explaining that if the cops came he could throw the cocaine into the water. They did, and as the exchange of the stolen property for the cocaine started to happen Kennedy said, "It's a done deal". The problem was, no one came. So, he told Glen D. that he was a police officer and that he was under arrest. Glen D. apparently did not want to be under arrest, so he reached under his coat and pulled out his pistol, at which time Kennedy shot him three times and he fell to the ground.

The covering officers had heard the code words and went to the "white house", saw that Kennedy's car was not there and then immediately drove down the dirt road to the scene, where they observed Kennedy with pistol in hand and Glen D. on the ground. An ambulance was summoned and Glen D. was transported to a local hospital. He was subsequently released to the Ashe County Sheriff's Department and placed in jail under a $150,000 bond.

In keeping with policy and procedure, I immediately called the ASAC to report the incident. He, in turn, notified the SAC, who then notified the Deputy Associate Director (Law Enforcement). The following day, a Shooting Review Team (ASAC Stanfill and me) was activated by the Associate Director to investigate and report on the incident to include "Factors Contributing To The Incident" and "Recommendations". Agents Warren and Driver prepared statements as to the incident, and I interviewed and took statements from the local officers involved. The ASAC interviewed Agents Driver and Warren.

The final report identified contributing factors to be the weather (rainy, extremely foggy with little or no light or visibility), failure of the transmitter in Kennedy's car so that the cover team did not here the last minute move to the stream, and probably the factor that most contributed to the incident was the last minute change itself, wherein Glen D. was allowed to dictate and control the situation rather than the officers. As to recommendations (relative to Warren and Driver's actions and involvement only), the report stated that they participated only as a part of a cover team and had no significant participation in the planning or directions of the investigation. Thusly, no ATF procedures or policy changes or additional training was recommended.

The report did note that they failed to obtain SAC approval relative to the utilization of props (the alleged stolen property) in accordance with established guidelines. However, upon being counseled by the ASAC relative to SAC approval prior to involvement in investigations where props are used by state and local officers, no further action was recommended. Case closed.

As in this case, when Warren and Driver got together two things seem to follow. First, something out of the ordinary was going to happen and secondly, a funny story about the incident would usually surface later. As Driver told the story, after the shots were heard and Kennedy was not where he was supposed to be, things became chaotic somewhat like the Keystone cops with officers scurrying about in the darkness and fog falling into and over one another.

Driver continued on, telling about the ASAC coming to interview him and Warren. He met with the ASAC first, and after a lengthy explanation as to what happened and the actions that he and Warren had taken, the ASAC said, "Driver, I think we can sum this up by saying the incident was a result of poor planning". Driver disagreed with the ASAC and once again explained what had happened and that he thought that the initial plan was good and that the movement of the take down location was the problem and caused the shooting incident.

The ASAC listened attentively according to Driver, but at the end again said, "I think we can sum this up as a case of poor planning". Driver disagreed again and explained why and this went on for about two hours, at which time he finally agreed it was "poor planning." Warren then went in with the ASAC and was out after about ten minutes. Driver was puzzled with Warren only being with the ASAC ten minutes, and asked him what he had told the ASAC. Warren said I told him, "It was just poor planning," and he agreed. (Warren had had his ear to the wall listening to the Driver/ASAC interview.)

HQ Detail

In January 1992, the SAC called me and told me he had to send a RAC to HQ for a 30-day detail and he had volunteered me to go. The previous year he had volunteered me to be a coordinator for a New Agent Training class at the ATF Academy in Georgia. After a lengthy explanation as to why it should not be me, I reluctantly said okay after he had assured me it was only temporary. I reported to HQ in February and was assigned to the Explosives Division and given a desk in an office with Agent Greg Plott, who I knew from his time at the Greeneville POD.

After a few days of settling in and meeting most of the guys, I realized I did not seem to have much to do. My only assignment was to learn how to prepare "briefing papers" on incidents involving ATF, which came in from the various field offices. The briefing paper was a brief, concise summary of the particular incident that would go forward up the chain of command to, I reckon, the Director, depending on the incident. At first glance, it appeared to be a relatively simple task of putting down what, who, where, how, and why. Not so. I learned that these papers were written, reviewed, rewritten and reviewed again by everyone in the office, sometimes taking all day to get it just right. Apparently, I got the hang of it and was allowed to participate and even write one that passed muster after only a couple re-writes.

As I sat there with little else to do, I was reminded of comments made by two agents regarding their experience in headquarters. Bill Behen, who came from DC to the SAC in Charlotte, characterized his time in DC as like being pecked to death by duck—slow and painful. Tom Dority, in reflecting on his time in DC, said you didn't have much to do but you had to look busy. He said his desk was always covered with files, reports and other various and assorted papers. And that on Friday afternoon he would gather everything up, put it in large envelopes, and mail them to himself, and when he got in Monday he would open the envelope and spread it all out again on his desk.

I asked if there was anything I could work on (to help pass the day). One of my supervisors informed me that there was a task that had been needing to be done for some time and took me to a small room filled with what appeared to be thousands of photographs, slides, negatives, and papers. Some were in boxes, envelopes, and folders, but most were just strewn about the room. He explained that they were from abortion clinic fire bombings and other fires and bombings worked by ATF over the year. My job, if I decided to take it, would be to go through everything and put them in some order so they could be used in presentations and training. I said I will do it, and spent pretty much my remaining time there devoted to the project. Some of the guys probably thought I was nuts, but I had to find something to do to pass the time. After all, you can only drink so much coffee and eat so many bear claws.

About a week or so before my time was up, Don Kincaid called me into his office and asked how things were going. I told him things were going okay, but I was glad the detail was about over and I would be going back to my POD. He seemed a little puzzled and said, "You know you are coming back on a Permanent Change of Station (PCS)," adding, "that is what you want, isn't it?"

It was then my turn to look a bit puzzled, and I quickly told him there had apparently been some misunderstanding and I did not want a PCS to HQ. Kincaid said they were under the impression that I had asked for the temporary assignment and wanted a PCS and added that he thought my PCS was already a "done deal". After convincing him I was volunteered for the temporary assignment and had no desire whatsoever to come to HQ, he said he would check on it.

A few days later he told me I should go in and talk with Mr. Brown, Chief of the Explosives Division. Mr. Brown reiterated that they were under the impression that I wanted to come to HQ, and he had recommended my PCS to HQ. I told him that I had no desire to come to HQ and was very happy in my current position and just wanted to finish my last two years there. He listened and seemed genuinely sympathetic to my situation, and finally said, "Okay, I will see what I can do."

He called me later that day or the next and said that I would not be transferred to HQ and wished me well.

Winston-Salem Task Force

Violent crime and gangs continued to be the focus nationally, as well as in the Charlotte Division. With the success of the Charlotte

ATF/local task force and the Raleigh Jamaican Task Force, there was a big push to establish an additional joint task force in the division. The SAC dictated that we establish a joint task force with the Winston-Salem Police Department.

Chief Sweat and I met several times to discuss establishing a joint task force to address the violent crime/gang problem in Winston-Salem. While he listened to our pitch, it was pretty obvious he was leery of the whole concept and hesitant to commit. Admittedly, I too, was a little skeptical, because unlike with the Charlotte Task Force, we (ATF) had very little money and resources other than bodies and of course the federal courts. In the end, Chief Sweat reluctantly agreed to participate, and we discussed procedures and guidelines. He furnished a room in the police department and committed two officers.

Special Agents Melton and Olson were assigned to the task force with assistance from other agents as needed. The plan called for all seized firearms to be traced and investigated, review and further investigate incident reports involving firearms, identify and investigate armed violent criminals and gang members, and pursue prosecution in federal court when appropriate. For a number of reasons, it became apparent after a few weeks it was not going to work. So, we agreed to disband the formal task force but continue to work together to address the violent crime on a case by case basis.

ATF-SBI-FBI Task Force

No sooner had we resolved the Winston-Salem task force situation, there was a push to create a violent offender task force with the SBI and the FBI. The push, as I recall, was from the powers-to-be in the SBI as well as ATF, and obviously from the FBI brass, although they did not usually participate in such things. In any event, a big meeting was held and all agreed this was the right thing to do. Unlike in the prior task force designated to one area, this would be a mobile task force going where needed and requested within the territorial jurisdiction of the Greensboro ATF, SBI and FBI. The SBI obtained office space and telephone service and all furnished desk and equipment. SBI Supervisor Edd Hunt and I oversaw and supervised the project. The SBI assigned Agent James Bowman, the FBI assigned Agent Dennis

Baker, and I assigned ATF Agents Olson, Melton, and Spann to the task force.

The first target was a gang of young armed drug dealers in Reidsville. Working with local officers, an investigation was opened to identify gang members and make cases against those violating the drug and firearms laws. Agents had some success, but as things progressed so did the problems.

The assigned FBI agent did not actively participate in the day-to- day work, but only attended meetings to get copies of reports to submit to his superiors. In fact, his supervisor told me that they (FBI) were not going to actively participate but just get the reports to send to their superiors. He went on to say they really didn't want to participate in the Task Force, but were forced to do so by their superiors so they could say that THE FBI was on the front lines in the fight against armed violent criminals and be able to take credit for any accomplishments. As one might imagine, SBI Supervisor Edd Hunt and I, as well as our assigned agents, didn't think too much of the arrangement. But to use a phrase I don't particularly like, it is (was) what it is (was), and you just accept it and move on.

Waco

February 28, 1993 was a very dark and deadly day for ATF. ATF agents attempted to serve a search warrant at the compound of the Branch Davidian religious sect near Waco, Texas. The Davidians resisted, and a violent firefight ensued that claimed the lives of six Davidians and four young ATF agents: Conway C. LeBleu, Todd W. McKeehan, Robert J. Williams, and Steven D. Willis. Following a fifty-one-day standoff between the Davidians and the FBI, a second assault was made on the compound that resulted in a massive fire that destroyed the compound and claimed the lives of seventy-six more Davidians including men, women and children and the sect leader Vernon Wayne Howell a/k/a David Koresh. After a number of reviews, inquiries, investigations, and volumes of reports, there still are questions and varying opinions as to how and why the massacre occurred and ultimately who was to blame for the deaths. To try to look at it objectively, I believe you have to separate the two events—the ATF raid and the FBI siege.

As to the ATF raid, the facts were: ATF, state, and local officers were conducting an investigation relative to violations of the federal firearms laws by the Davidians, including the possession of automatic weapons. The investigation was also directed at alleged child abuse and false imprisonment by Koresh.

An ATF undercover agent infiltrated the group and confirmed the firearms violations. ATF officials decided to conduct a surprise raid on the compound with federal search warrants. They devised a plan to approach the compound concealed in horse trailers. When the agents got out of the trailers, knocked on the door announcing their presence and intent to serve the search warrants, shots were fired and the shootout began. ATF agents insist that they were shot on first from someone inside the compound, and the Davidians and their allies and sympathizers say it was the ATF who first fired. Generally, there are two questions that arise regarding the ATF action. The first being should the ATF raid had taken place at all and secondly, once the element of surprise was gone should they have continued with the search warrants.

Some say that ATF and local officers should have just arrested Koresh in town or somewhere away from the compound. As I understand it at the time, Koresh was no longer going into town or leaving the compound at all. More importantly, the purpose of the raid was to not only arrest Koresh, but to search for illegal firearms and explosives and other evidence of criminal violations of the law. That could only be accomplished by a consent search or by the execution of search warrants. I don't see Koresh consenting to a search of the compound.

An ATF undercover agent was in the compound just before the raid and found out that Koresh had been warned, "the ATF are coming". He then informed the raid agents that Koresh knew they were coming. The leaders of the raid team decided to continue with the raid and hurried things along. Did they understand that "the ATF are coming" meant right now or the next day, next week or what? To me that is a crucial point.

Knowing what we know now, if the raid leaders fully understood that it meant, "He knows we are coming right now," then the element of surprise was gone and the raid should have been called off. The problem with that is that the raid leaders didn't know then what we know now. They had to make their decision in real time with the information they had at the time. And I suspect that the amount of time, money, and effort already invested in the investigation might have been a factor and made it very difficult to just call it off.

The assault on the compound by the FBI came after fifty-one days of trying to negotiate with Koresh to bring about a peaceful resolution to the standoff. I think they did everything possible to resolve the standoff so that no one would be hurt or killed including the men, women and children in the compound. What else could they have done to appease Koresh? Surely, Koresh didn't think they were just going away after he and some of his followers had just murdered four young ATF agents. And when they did assault the compound the evidence clearly shows that the ensuing fire was actually set from inside with multiple points of origin found.

In both actions, looking back there is no doubt that some things could have been done differently that might have changed or lessened the disastrous outcome. But the agents making the decisions then did not have that luxury, and I believe they did what they thought was best at the time. David Koresh was the only person that could have prevented the death and destruction, and in my mind is solely responsible for the ultimate outcome, one that I think he wanted.

As a result of the Waco raid and aftermath, ATF Director Steve Higgins and Associate Director Dan Hartnett were forced to retire and disciplinary actions were taken against others involved in the planning and execution of the raid. John Magaw, a former Director of the USSS, was appointed ATF Director.

Greensboro ATF Office Opened

On July 1, 1993, the relocation of the ATF Office from Winston-Salem to 1801 Stanley Road, Greensboro was completed. The new office, located in a commercial building, was much nicer and spacious than the federal building in Winston-Salem. There were individual offices for the agents and ample parking close to the building for everyone. The relocation had been a very long and often frustrating process, and everyone was glad it was over and things could return to some normalcy and permanency.

ATF – FBI Merger

The move to abolish ATF again surfaced in the fall of 1993. In published newspaper reports in September, Arizona Senator DeConcini, a strong ATF supporter, said he expected the Clinton administration to merge ATF with FBI within eighteen months. He stated that it was going to happen because ATF's boss, Treasury Secretary Lloyd Benson, did not oppose and in fact backed the merger plan. The ATF-FBI merger proposal was a part of Vice President Gore's "reinventing government" plan, which also included moving DEA into the FBI. Fortunately, there was opposition from a number of federal, state, and local law enforcement groups and members of Congress. For whatever reasons, like before it did not come to fruition and ATF survived once again

Brady Law

The Brady Law was passed in 1993 primarily as a result of the efforts of Jim and Sarah Brady. Jim Brady was shot in 1982 in the attempted assassination of President Ronald Reagan by John Hinkley, and suffered permanent brain damage and disabilities. He, his wife, and others campaigned for years to get the bill passed. The Brady Law established a national waiting period and a criminal history check for purchasers of firearms. It also raised license fees and made the theft of guns from a Federal Firearms Licensee a federal violation.

Federal Crime Bill of 1994

The bill banned the manufacture, importation, and transfer of assault weapons and large capacity clips. The law also added an additional class of prohibited persons by making persons subject to restraining orders prohibited from receive or possess a firearm.

Chapter Nineteen
THE END

King Solomon, the wisest man in the world, wrote in Ecclesiastes 3:1—"There is time for everything, and a season for every activity under the heavens."

While he did not include there is a time to retire, for most people that time does come. For a federal law enforcement agent (GS-1811), that time comes between the ages of 50 and 57. Under the Civil Service Retirement System an agent with twenty years of service is eligible for retirement at the age of 50 and it is mandatory at age 57. A few go at 50 and some stay on until the mandatory 57, but the majority retire somewhere in between.

When to retire of course depends on the individual and his circumstances. If you are still making cases or otherwise contributing and enjoying the job there is no reason to retire early. On the other hand, if you have lost interest in the job and are no longer contributing anything or have some other need to retire early then do it. Over the course of my twenty-five years, I had seen a number of agents who stayed on much too long. They become disillusioned and unhappy with the job, feel that they have been victimized by someone or the system, and just quit doing their job. They know that short of murder or high treason they can't be fired or made to work, and for management it easier to just accept it rather than trying to take some corrective action.

Having observed and experienced the "disgruntled/victimized employee condition" a number of times, I vowed early on that when my time came I would hopefully recognize it and go. It was while on detail in HQ that I really started to think about going out at 50. After all, I couldn't go back on my word to Mr. Brown that I was going to retire in two years when he was considering my transfer to HQ. Without going into any pointless details, I came to the conclusion that events and circumstances were such that it was probably time for me to go. I just wasn't having fun anymore and the **"Moonshiner and Revenuer" days were never coming back**.

On February 25, 1994, Special Agent James (Jim) J. Roche, Jr. retired from the Federal Bureau of Investigation after more than thirty years of distinguished service. That night I attended a retirement party held in his honor at the Prestonwood Country Club in Cary, North Carolina. On March 11, 1994, only two weeks into his retirement, Jim died of a heart attack.

On October 4, 1994, shortly after my 50th birthday, I retired from the Bureau of Alcohol, Tobacco, and Firearms after twenty-eight years of government service.

I Remember

Though dead and gone, in my memory you remain
And come alive again each time I recall your name

Mike Zetts, *ATF Agent*
Oscar Vaughan, *ATF Agent*
Bill Walden, *ATF Agent*
D. C. Williams, *Raleigh Police Officer*
Dale Winters, *ATF Agent*
John Wurtele, *ATF Agent*
Haywood Weddle, *ATF Agent*
Deborah West, *ATF Agent*
Bill Terrell, *ATF Agent*
Tommy Stokes, *ATF Agent*
Bill Sparkman, *Wake County ABC Officer*
Bobby Sherrill, *ATF Agent*
Herb Steely, *ATF Agent*
Charlie Smith, *ATF Agent*
Jim Roche, *FBI Agent*
John Rice, *ATF Agent*
Marvin Shaw, *ATF Agent*
Charlie Turner, *Durham County ABC Officer*
Bill Queen, Sr., *ATF Agent*
Lewis Phillips, *Siler City Police Chief*
Chuck Poole, *Federal Protective Service Officer (USMC Retired)*
Bob Powell, *ATF Agent*
L.C. Puryear, *ATF Agent*
Stan Noel, *ATF Agent*
Bill Maine, *ATF Agent*
Leonard Mika, *ATF Agent*
Bob Martin, *ATF Agent*
Larry Morrissey, *ATF Agent*
Jack Medlin, *Executive, Liggett and Myers Tobacco Company*
Butch Madden, *FBI Agent*
Jim Lancaster, *ATF Agent*
Roland Leary, *Durham County ABC Chief/Sheriff*
Frank Lee, *ATF Agent*
Mark Lynch, *N.C. Secretary of Revenue*
Pat Kelly, *ATF Agent*
Jim Kegley, *ATF Agent*

Jim King, *ATF Agent*
Steve Jones, *SBI Agent*
Bob Izzo, *ATF/Customs Agent*
Bud Hazelip, *ATF Agent*
Betty Haley, *ATF Secretary*
Ray Hart, *ATF Agent*
Fred Heineman, *Raleigh Police Chief/US Congressman*
Bob Holland, *ATF Agent*
Warren Hilton, *ATF Agent*
Joe Hines, *SBI Agent*
Agnes Hunter, *ATF Secretary to SAC*
Maurice Gettleman, *ATF Agent*
M.L. Goodwin, *ATF Agent*
Bob Furr, *ATF Agent*
Al Felton, *NC ALE/DMV Officer*
Tony Ferguson, *ATF Agent*
Kolen Flack, *ATF Agent*
Charlie Foxworth, *ATF Agent*
Ralph Ellis, *ATF Agent*
Jack Elkins, *Chatham County Sheriff*
Dave Edmisten, *ATF Agent*
William Dement, *Franklin County Sheriff*
Tom Dority, *ATF Agent*
Gene Calcote, *ATF Agent*
Joe Carter, *ATF Agent*
Burch Compton, *Orange County ABC Chief*
Arthur Ray Currin, *Granville County ABC Chief/Sheriff*
Bubba Council, *ATF Agent*
Paul Cook, *Orange County ABC Officer*
James Barefoot, *Johnston County ABC Chief*
Earl Blake, *ATF Agent*
Bull Blettner, *ATF Agent*
Bob Bowen, *ATF Agent*
Johnny Bouras, *ATF Agent*
Ken Brady, *ATF Agent*
Jim Bright, *ATF Regional Counsel*
Henry Byrd, *ATF Agent*
Garland Bunting, *Halifax ABC Chief*
Ralph Anthony, *ATF Officer*
Don Andrews, *AFT Agent*
Perry Anderson, *ATF Agent*

ACKNOWLEDGMENTS

The author wishes to acknowledge and thank the following individuals for their help and assistance in the writing of this book:

W. H. "Buzzy" Anthony, Stewart, Florida
Steve Barrow, Kittrell, North Carolina
Bill Belvin, Mooresville, North Carolina
Phil Carter, Midland, North Carolina
Gary Cunard, Louisburg, North Carolina
Billy Dement, Louisburg, North Carolina
Charlie Favre, Lexington, North Carolina
Ed Garrison, Raleigh, North Carolina
Stephen Hodgkins, Knightdale, North Carolina
Todd Johnson, Smithfield, North Carolina
Dave McAleer, Garner, North Carolina
Neta Rice, St. Simons Island, Georgia
Frank Stephenson Jr., Murfreesboro, North Carolina

ABOUT THE AUTHOR

Johnny Binkley was born and grew up in Chatham County, a rural county in central North Carolina. Growing up on a farm, he learned early on the necessity and value of hard work. After high school, he joined the army during the time of the Cuban Missile crisis. After basic training in Georgia, he was stationed in Maryland at the Edgewood Arsenal and later in Utah at the Dugway Proving Grounds.

After his three-year tour, he returned to North Carolina and attended Pembroke State University, and graduating in 1969 with a degree in Political Science. Immediately upon graduation, he went to work as a Special Investigator with the federal Alcohol, Tobacco, and Firearms Division of the Internal Revenue Service. He was fortunate to be stationed in North Carolina his entire twenty-five-year career — Raleigh (twice), Charlotte, Winston-Salem, and Greensboro. He retired in October 1994 as the Resident Agent in Charge of the Greensboro field office.

After his retirement, he worked briefly for a security and consulting company in Raleigh, and later was self-employed as a contract investigator for several private firms and government agencies.

His wife of fifty-six years, Charlene, and he live in Raleigh with frequent trips to the beach at Emerald Isle. They have two grown children, John and Angie, and four grandchildren, Jensen (19), Reagan (16), Charlie (10), and Cate-Hill (8). His time now is pretty much spent around family and volunteering at his church. He gets together with a few of the "old revenuers" in the area for lunch about every week.

INDEX

G

Gardner, Ava 54, 94
Garner, Dick 126
Garrison, Ed 50, 71, 79, 127, 128, 136, 141, 151, 164, 165, 176, 190, 193, 198, 214, 216, 228, 245
Gazzola, Robert V. 91
German Central Farm 204
Gettleman, Maurice 244
Glascoe, Janet 228, 230
Glynco, Georgia 20, 124
Goldsboro, North Carolina 23, 131
Goodwin, M.L. 17, 115, 244
Gore, Al 240
Graham, Bob 99, 159, 202
Granville County, North Carolina 25, 40, 44, 59, 77, 79, 82, 108, 112, 122, 132, 166
Graves, Sheriff 111
Gray, Ed 19, 45
Gray, John Ross 69
Greensboro, North Carolina 23, 128, 131, 136, 187, 222, 229, 239
Greenville, South Carolina 137, 205
Greenville, Tennessee 137
Griffin, William N. (Bill) 23, 24, 65, 100, 118, 130, 138
Gun Control Act of 1968 (GCA of 1968) 21, 25, 56, 57, 110, 119, 134, 197, 198, 209
Gupton, Lloyd 33, 83, 86, 169

H

Haley, Betty 19, 105, 244
Halifax County, North Carolina 117
Hall, Linwood 122
Harnett County, North Carolina 166, 167
Harris, Herman 32, 88
Harris, Michael 126, 127
Hartnett, Dan 219, 239
Hart, Ray 244
Hazelip, Bud 244
Hearn, Lance 126
Heineman, Fred 244
Hells Angel Motorcycle Club (HAMC) 160, 220, 229
Henderson, Al 62
Henderson, Leon 62
Henderson, North Carolina 59, 95, 112, 139
Hickory, North Carolina 23, 131
Higgins, Stephen E. (Steve) 195, 239

High South Interstate Drug Task Force 231
Hilton, Warren 105, 244
Hines, Joe 182, 194, 244
Hinkley, John 187, 240
Hodgkins, Stephen 245
Holland, Bob 244
Hoover, J. Edgar 45
Hope, Bob 207
Hopkins, Mike 137
Horton, Kenneth 61, 96
Horton, Tom 111
Howell, Vernon Wayne 237
Hughes, Ed 124
Hunt, Edd 236, 237
Hunter, Agnes 18, 244
Hunt, James B. 149, 184
Hutson, Richard 96

I

Immigration and Naturalization Service 223
Ingleside, North Carolina 33
Internal Revenue Service 22
International Response Team (ITR) 159
Ivey, William 122
Izzo, Bob 244

J

Jackson, Julius 48
Jefferson County, Tennessee 115
Jeffrey, William Andrew 120
Jeffries, Tommy 75
Johnson, Allen Ray 69
Johnson, Arthur 169
Johnson, Calvin 69
Johnson, Henry 48
Johnson, Junior 50, 118
Johnsons Restaurant 128
Johnson, Todd 245
Johnston County, North Carolina 25, 32, 50, 51, 54, 73, 94, 113, 114, 132, 136
Jones, Steve 244
J.W. Perry's Store 133

K

Kearney, Synthia 190
Keathley, Miles 157
Kegley, Jim 243
Keith, Mr. 112
Keith Store 112

North Carolina State Bureau of
Investigation (SBI) 17, 125, 160,
194, 223, 225, 226, 236

O

Ohio State University 206
Olson, Chris 228, 229, 236, 237
O'Neal, Curtis Lee 59
Operation Dry Up 24
Orange County, North Carolina 25,
61, 96, 125
Organized Crime Control Act of
1970 198
Organized Crime Drug Task Force
(OCDETF) 223
Osborne, Barbara 230
Outlaw Motorcycle Club (OMC)
221
Oxford, North Carolina 39, 57

P

Palmdale, California 206
Parkersburg, West Virginia 206
Parma, Ohio 204
Pate, Andy 137
Pearce, Gary 149
Pembroke State University 17
Peoples, Linwood 41
Percy Flowers Store 52, 54, 94
Perquimans County, North Carolina
136
Perry, James 112
Perry, J.W. 134
Person County, North Carolina 25,
111
Phillips, Lewis 243
Pierce, Larry 216
Piggly Wiggly 225
Pines 39, 40, 41, 44
Pistole, Jerry 140
Planters Oil Mill 202
Pleasants, Fleming Macon 60
Pleasants Jr., Coy 60, 87, 102, 170
Plemmons, Newt 187
Plott, Greg 234
Pollard, Randy 156
Poole, Chuck 243
Poole, Harold 104
Poole, Reed 69, 103
Powell, Bob 65, 86, 118, 122, 137,
182, 243
Powell, Steve 118
Preacher, The 43, 44, 53

Pritchett, Tommy 122
Project CUE (Concentrated Urban
Enforcement) 130
Puryear, L.C. 75, 243

Q

Queen, Sr., Bill 90, 243

R

Raleigh Fire Department 188, 214
Raleigh Jamaican Task Force 223,
236
Raleigh News and Observer 155
Raleigh, North Carolina 7, 18, 23,
25, 35, 49, 50, 113, 116, 117,
132, 139, 140, 144, 153, 156,
159, 161, 193, 205, 210, 219
Raleigh Police Department 99,
223, 224
Reagan, Mrs. 205
Reagan, Ronald 8, 50, 187, 195,
204, 205, 206, 207, 240
Reams, Milton 199
Reece, Marshall 60, 115, 122, 127,
151
Reedy, Timothy 143
Rice, John 243
Rice, Neta 183, 245
Roanoke Rapids, North Carolina
147, 151
Robbins, Parker 84
Roberts, Jim 137, 216
Robeson County, North Carolina
110
Robinson, Jerry 154
Roche, Jr., James (Jim) 211, 242,
243
Rochester, New York 206
Rockwell International Test
Installation 206
Rocky Ford, North Carolina 120
Rocky Mount, North Carolina 23,
64, 97, 117, 130, 132, 199, 202
Rogers, Dennis 117
Ross, Doug 39, 41, 42, 44, 47, 69,
83, 97, 98, 211, 212
Rougemont, North Carolina 103

S

Salisbury, North Carolina 23, 122,
131
Sanders, Bob 157
Sanford, North Carolina 153

War Memorial Auditorium 206
Warren County, North Carolina 25, 62, 121
Warren, Ted 228, 229, 232, 233
Washington, DC 20
Watkins, Bill 58
Watson, Donald 122
Webb, Bill 215, 224
Weddle, Haywood 90, 243
Weems, Charlie 122, 126
Weinman, Paul 229
Weldon, North Carolina 147
Wenner, Doug 228
West, Deborah 228, 229, 230, 243
West, John 100, 115, 123
Westra, John 124, 135, 139, 140, 141, 143, 148, 158, 198, 219
Whaley, George 69
White, Larry 221, 222
White Level, North Carolina 109, 111, 120
White Oak Baptist Church 50
Whitlow, Steve 124, 135, 141, 219
Wiggins, Dick 140
Wigglesworth, Bill 156
Wilder's Store 59
Wilkesboro, North Carolina 19, 23, 50, 118, 119, 131, 137
Wilkesboro Olympians 122, 123
Wilkes County, North Carolina 19, 37, 59, 61, 62, 118, 166, 211
Wilkinson, Alec 117
Williams, D. C. 243
Williams, Dwight 69

Williams, Plessy 20
Williams, Robert J. 237
Williams, Ronnie 65, 86, 113, 166, 182
Williamston, North Carolina 23, 130
Willis, Steven D. 237
Wilmington, North Carolina 23, 39, 228
Wilson, Joe 151
Wilson, North Carolina 159, 226
Winchester, Virginia 151
Winston-Salem, North Carolina 23, 228, 229, 230, 236
Winston-Salem Police Department 236
Winston-Salem Task Force 235
Winters, Dale 140, 219, 243
Woodham, Earl 190
Wurtele, John 18, 23, 243

Y

Yadkin County, North Carolina 38, 39, 47
Youngsville, North Carolina 60, 99, 120

Z

Zetts, Anita 135
Zetts, Mike 19, 30, 32, 33, 34, 35, 38, 41, 45, 62, 65, 74, 81, 87, 98, 109, 111, 117, 124, 133, 134, 135, 136, 174, 243
Zimmerman, Donald 91

See More Great Books

at

WWW.ACCLAIMPRESS.COM

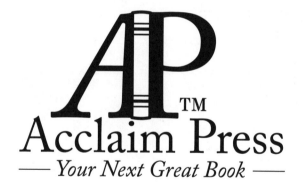